MY TIME WITH GOD

150 Ways to Start Your Own Quiet Time

MY TIME WITH GOD

150 Ways to Start Your Own Quiet Time

by
Jeanette Dall
Carla Williams
B. J. Bassett

Tyndale House Publishers, Wheaton, Illinois

Heritage Builders

MY TIME WITH GOD

Library of Congress Cataloging-in-Publication Data

Dall, Jeanette.
My time with God : 150 ways to start your own quiet time / by
Jeanette Dall, Carla Williams, B.J Bassett.
p. cm. — (Heritage builders)
"A Focus on the Family book"—T.p. verso.
Includes bibliographical references and index.
Summary: A collection of 150 devotionals that give the reader
the opportunity to spend quiet time with God. Includes suggested
readings from the Old and New Testaments, prayer starters, questions
to ponder, and facts and fun from the Bible.
ISBN 1–56179–802–9
1. Teenagers—Prayer-books and devotions—English. 2. Bible—
Devotional use. [1. Prayer books and devotions. 2. Christian life.] I.
Williams, Carla. II. Bassett, B.J. III. Title. IV. Series.

BV4850 .D35 2000
242'.63—dc21

00–021068

A Focus on the Family book published by Tyndale House Publishers,
Wheaton, Illinois.

For Lightwave
Concept Design and Direction: Rick Osborne
Managing Editor: Elaine Osborne
Text Director: K. Christie Bowler
Art Director: Terry Van Roon
Desktop Publisher: Andrew Jaster
Editorial Assistants: Mikal Clarke, Ed Strauss

Cover Design: Steve Diggs & Friends, Nashville

Printed in the United States of America

03 04 05/10 9 8 7 6 5

CONTENTS

What Are Times with God and What's Their Point? 7

How Do You Do Quiet Times? 8

What to Expect and How to Use This Book 10

The Greatest Story 12

The Old Testament

Genesis 15

Exodus–Deuteronomy 37

Joshua 61

Judges 69

Ruth 75

1 & 2 Samuel 79

1 & 2 Kings 99

Ezra & Nehemiah 121

Esther 127

The New Testament

The Gospels: Luke and John 131

Acts 169

Romans 187

Creative Ideas for Times with God 193

Suggestions for Extra Things to Do During Your
Times with God 196

An Index of Exciting Reads! 198

Reading by the Book 200

Topical Index 202

WHAT ARE TIMES WITH GOD AND WHAT'S THEIR POINT?

Is there a lot of noise in your life—telephone ringing, TV blaring, boom box booming, and computers buzzing and beeping? And how about the people coming and going— talking, singing, laughing, slamming doors, and rattling dishes? Maybe there's even a cat or dog making its own kind of noise and commotion. This is pretty normal for a busy family; maybe a family just like yours.

But there are also times that aren't so noisy and busy. These are times to sit and think or dream, maybe even make great plans for what you would like to do in the future. That's a good time to find a quiet corner and use this book. *My Time with God* will help you know what God is like and help you build a truly awesome relationship with Him.

You and God

It takes two to have a relationship. You get to know people by talking with them and sharing your thoughts and ideas. It's the same way with God. You can get to know God by spending time with Him and sharing your joys, sorrows, worries, and big ideas. *My Time with God* will guide you in developing this wonderful relationship through Bible readings and questions, prayers, and fun ideas.

Bible Readings

God speaks to you through the Bible. It is His love letter telling you about Himself and all the things He does for you. The Bible also shows you how to lead a life that pleases God. In *My Time with God* you will find verses to read in God's Word, the Bible, and interesting questions asking about what you have read. You can also learn how the Bible teachings have meaning in your life right now!

Prayers

You can talk to God through prayer. This is where you can share everything in your heart and mind with God. God is an excellent listener, and He always hears you. Better than that, God can always help you with your problems or worries. Do you sometimes feel like you don't know what to say? Don't worry. *My Time with God* will give you prayer starters and ideas to help you as you talk to your heavenly Father. But don't feel limited to those. In fact, add the prayer starters to the other things you pray about, such as friends and family, needs you know about, or requests for help on your tests. God wants to know all about what you care about and to help you with it all.

Fun Ideas

Good relationships are full of joy and fun. You will find some of that in *My Time with God*, too. You can chuckle at a joke, learn some way-out trivia, or figure out a riddle.

So where's your quiet place going to be where you can have a great time with God?

HOW DO YOU DO QUIET TIMES!

When and where can you spend quiet time with God? The answer is anytime, anywhere. Well, *almost* anytime. If you're in the outfield, the bases are loaded, the bat connects with the ball, the crowd goes wild in the stands, and you're running for all you're worth, you *can* still pray a quick prayer, but this is *not* the best time to open your Bible, sit down on the grass, and quietly listen to God.

A Special Place

Spending quiet time with God takes concentration; so you'll need to find a place where you can focus on Him and His Word. Many Christians call this time "devotions" because it's *devoting* time and attention to God.

A good time for it is first thing in the morning, before your day begins. But you can have quiet times in your backyard after school, on a hilltop, on a beach, 10,000 feet above the earth in a hot air balloon—just about *anywhere* ('cause God's everywhere)! If you don't own a hot air balloon, you can always go to your bedroom after supper. In fact, the Bible says, "When you pray, go into your room, close the door" (Matthew 6:6).

It's About God

In your special place, focus on God, realizing just how awesome He is. As Psalm 46:10 says, "Be still, and know that I am God." It takes *time* to get perfectly still, shove all the busy thoughts out of your mind, and focus your heart on God who loves you. So you might start with prayer. Remember, prayer is about a relationship with God. It's you talking to Him and Him responding to you. His response could be helping you understand the Bible or your situation, or giving you a sense of peace or a new way to deal with something. If things aren't quite right between you and God, get that taken care of.

When you've offended a friend, the first thing you need to do when you meet again is make things right. So check out your heart (Psalm 4:4; 139:23–24) and ask Him to show you anything in your life He wants to change.

Then open this book and your Bible. Reading the Bible thoughtfully and asking questions about what you read is a great way to focus on God. Not only do you learn interesting, amazing, and wonderful things, but as you read, your thoughts are on God and His ways—it becomes even easier to talk to Him. God uses the Bible (His book!) to speak to you and answer your questions, telling you how much He loves you and how much you need Him. Reading the Bible and praying are great steps toward giving God control over your thoughts and life. And that's what it's all about!

WHAT TO EXPECT AND HOW TO USE THIS BOOK

The Bible is not simply a collection of scattered stories. The writers of the Bible all contributed to tell one *big story*. Down through history, from Adam and Eve in the Garden of Eden to Christ on the cross, from Moses on Mount Sinai to the apostle Paul in Rome, God has been unfolding a special plan. *My Time with God* is designed to help you see God's special plan for your life and to give you hours of fun and interesting reading as you draw close to God.

About This Book

When you're comfortably seated in a corner with your Bible, a notebook, and this book, you'll want to know how the book works. *My Time with God* is divided into sections for individual books of the Bible or a group of related books. At the beginning of each section is a fun and factual introduction explaining what that book of the Bible or section is about. Read this introduction, then start right in with your first day's reading.

The Starters

Each page or devotion helps you look at Bible stories from several different angles. These are quiet time starters since they get you started spending a quiet time with God.

At the top of the page, in the first few sentences, are some Bible references. Be sure to look up and read those verses in your Bible. Then look at *Think About It*. This gives thoughts about your Bible reading and asks questions about what you've just read to get you thinking about it and what it means to you. Take the time to answer them, because this is really what it's all about—finding out what God's saying in His Word and then living it out.

Go Deeper is for those of you who want to read more about the story or the day's topic. It gives you other related Bible verses to look up.

Prayer Starter provides a suggestion to start your prayer time off with. Use this, but pray about other things too—such as your family and friends, and whatever is on your heart.

Facts and Fun is usually related to the topic, but sometimes just contains jokes, trivia, quizzes, and interesting information that's, well, just for fun.

Coming Up Next hints at what you'll find on the following page.

Your Choice

You can use this book different ways. You can read it like we've just explained, or you can read it by *topic*. Say you want to learn about who Jesus is. Go to the *Topical Index* in the back of the book, look up "Jesus" alphabetically, then go to the page numbers listed and do those quiet time starters. You could also just choose a book you're interested in, say Esther or Exodus, and do those starters so that you get a good understanding of that book. If you get into a rut, check out *Creative Ideas for Times with God* or *An Index of Exciting Reads* at the back of this book. Whatever you choose, have fun and meet with God!

THE GREATEST STORY

The Bible tells one big story about God and His desire to have a wonderful relationship with us. It all began when only God existed—God the Father, Son, and Holy Spirit . . .

GENESIS

God made everything, including the first people, Adam and Eve. He gave them a beautiful garden to live in with only one rule: Don't eat fruit from a certain tree. Because they disobeyed God, however, He sent them out of the garden. Their sin separated them from God, and everyone born since then has also been born sinful and separated from God. The penalty for sin is death, but God had a plan to bring us back to Him. In the meantime, when they sinned, God told His people to sacrifice (kill) lambs to pay for those sins.

Several thousand years ago, God chose a man named Abraham and told Abraham He'd be his God. He called Abraham out of Mesopotamia into the land of Canaan and promised to give the land to Abraham's descendants forever. Some years after Abraham and his wife arrived in Canaan, they had a son named Isaac.

Isaac's son Jacob, or *Israel*, had twelve sons, but Joseph was his favorite. Joseph's brothers were jealous and sold him as a slave into Egypt. Much later, God showed Joseph that a terrible famine was coming, and knowing that made him one of the most powerful men in Egypt. When Joseph's family came for food, Joseph invited them to live in Egypt.

EXODUS-DEUTERONOMY

The children of Israel were called *Israelites*, and after many years, they'd become very numerous. So numerous that a new Pharaoh decided to do something about it. First, he made them slaves; then he ordered their newborn boys killed. But God had a plan, and Pharaoh's own daughter rescued an Israelite baby, Moses, and raised him in the palace.

Moses killed a man and had to flee into the desert. There God appeared to him and said, "Tell Pharaoh to let My people go!" Moses returned to Egypt with the message, but Pharaoh refused to listen, so God sent ten plagues to show that He was stronger than the false gods of Egypt. In the final plague the eldest child in every family died. But the Israelites sacrificed lambs and put the blood on their doorways so the angel of death would pass over their houses. This was called the *Passover*.

That night Pharaoh finally let the Israelites go, and they all left in one big "grand exit" that's called an *exodus*. God led them into the desert and, at Mount Sinai, gave Moses the *Ten Commandments* and the *Law*, which told the Israelites how to obey Him and live. Then God led them to Canaan, the land He'd promised to Abraham.

JOSHUA-JUDGES

After Moses died, Joshua took his place. Under Joshua's leadership, the Israelites defeated the wicked people living in Canaan and settled in. When the Israelites followed God's Law, things went well, but when they didn't, their enemies conquered them. They'd cry to God for help, and God would send a *judge,* or leader, to defeat their enemies.

1 SAMUEL-2 KINGS

Years later the Israelites asked God for a king, and their first king was Saul. After Saul died, David became king, and he loved God with all his heart. David's son Solomon was wise, but later kings didn't follow God's Law, so God sent *prophets* to warn them. Because they refused to listen, He let enemies take the Israelites as prisoners to distant Babylon.

EZRA-NEHEMIAH

Seventy years later, King Cyrus let the Jews return to their land and rebuild their city and temple. God's people finally decided to obey His Law, and then everything was ready for the key part of God's plan!

LUKE-JOHN

One day a young woman named Mary had a son named Jesus. Jesus was God's own Son, the promised Messiah, but He became a person like us because He loved us. When He was about thirty, Jesus began to teach about God and His kingdom. He showed that God loved people by healing the sick and feeding the hungry, and He taught how to have a good relationship with God.

The religious leaders were afraid the people would follow Jesus instead of them, so they paid Judas, one of Jesus' disciples, to lead guards to Jesus during the Passover. Jesus was arrested and tried for claiming He was God's Son, and then sentenced to be crucified. Crucifixion was a horrible death. Jesus was the ultimate Passover Lamb, and God accepted His death (instead of ours) as payment for our sins.

After Jesus died, His disciples put His body in a nearby tomb. But on the third day the tomb was empty! Jesus appeared to many of His disciples, proving that He was alive again.

ACTS-ROMANS

Jesus sent the Holy Spirit to help His disciples tell the world about Him. One religious leader, Saul, mistreated Jesus' disciples. But after Jesus appeared to Saul, Saul became one of Jesus' most famous disciples. Saul changed his name to Paul and traveled around the world telling people about Jesus. Paul wrote letters to help new believers live as God wanted them to.

Of course, we haven't included all of Paul's letters, or even every book of the Bible, in this book. There just wasn't room. But this book was created to help you get the big—the *really BIG*—picture that the Bible contains. And what a picture! What a story! The Bible tells the best true story ever written. GUARANTEED!

Grab your backpack and don't forget to pack a camera, a swimsuit, a sack lunch, and hiking boots. You'll need them. A video camera would even be better, because you're going on a big adventure and you'll want to capture the action!

You'll see God create the world out of nothing! And to your amazement, right before your eyes, God will create Adam from the dust of the ground, of all things. You'll witness the first surgery as God makes Eve from Adam's rib. Can you believe it? Well, it's true—all true.

From Sin to Salvation

OOPS! After all the good stuff comes a major problem in the Garden of Eden—a big mistake—sin!—that changed the world into a dark and dangerous place. But God had a plan to make things right again.

Genesis is a book of firsts. It's the beginning of the world and the beginning of life. It's the beginning of sin and the beginning of salvation. The purpose of God's creation was to share His love. Genesis is only the beginning of God's wonderful plan to rescue sinners and make us all His children.

Although God punishes sin, He is also faithful, loving, and caring toward His creation. He chose people like Noah, Abraham, Isaac, Jacob, and Joseph to do His will. In Genesis God shows you how to trust His promises and obey His plan.

Remember the swimsuit you packed? You'll need it when you climb aboard Noah's big boat. Those hiking boots are to trudge up the mountain with Abraham and Isaac. And that sack lunch will come in handy during the big famine.

Genesis Facts

Here are some interesting facts before you start on your great adventure. Moses is the author of the book of Genesis. Raised as an Egyptian, he was taught how to write and to understand the records and writings of that time. Moses is a great example of faithfulness, obedience, and following God's will.

Genesis is the first book in the Old Testament and one of the five books Moses wrote, which the Jews call the *Torah.* The five books of Moses are Genesis, Exodus, Leviticus, Numbers, and Deuteronomy. Genesis contains 50 chapters and some of the most famous stories in the Bible.

AW, IT WAS NOTHING!

Did you ever wonder how something could come out of nothing? How did the world, or all the universe for that matter, come into existence? Where did all the amazing plants and animals come from? Read Genesis 1:1–27 for some answers.

Think About It

- If you could help God create the animals, what type of animal would you create? Why?
- Would you have made other planets in our solar system for people to live on too? Why?
- Close your eyes and try to think of nothingness—no light, no walls, no stars. Now think of a great voice saying, "Let there be light!" How does the picture change?

Go Deeper

Read Genesis 1:28–2:3; Isaiah 45:12, 18; Job 38:1–11; Hebrews 11:1–3.

Prayer Starter

God can do absolutely anything! He just said the word and things came into existence. *Cool!* And now He wants to be your Father and Friend? Talk to God about that and anything else you want.

Facts and Fun

Where is the Big Dipper? Can you see the Milky Way? Which is your favorite planet besides Earth? Why? Isn't it amazing to think that God made it all?

Coming Up Next

Did you ever want to live on an absolutely perfect planet? Next time, learn about people who actually did!

Who created the heavens + the earth

CREATION/GOD IS ALL-POWERFUL

How did God do it

17

What did God make it out of

all things were ___

JUST CALL ME DUSTY

God created an entire universe of galaxies, suns, and stars. God also made a beautiful world filled with plants and animals. Everything was perfect. Only one more thing was needed. Read Genesis 2:4–25 to find out what it was.

Think About It

- God placed Adam in the Garden of Eden. What was so special about this garden? How did putting Adam there show God's care for him?
- What did God do for Adam when Adam was lonely?
- In what ways is *your* home just what you need? What "do not touch" rules do you have?

Go Deeper

Read Psalm 68:6a; Mark 10:6–9; Romans 8:32; 1 Corinthians 15:45–49.

Prayer Starter

God understands your needs too. Thank Him for all the things He has given you that are just perfect for you.

Facts and Fun

Many people think the Garden of Eden was in modern-day Iraq. Wherever the Garden was, no one knows where it *went* to. It's gone! Vanished! Not a trace has ever been found. Some people believe it was wiped out by the great Flood in the days of Noah.

Coming Up Next

Did you ever have something that was perfect, but then it got wrecked or lost? Next time, learn about people who lost all their privileges and got into big trouble!

KICKED OUT

Have you ever gotten too wild in a playground and had your privilege of playing there taken away? Read about the very first disobedience and punishment in Genesis 3:1–24.

Think About It

- How would things have been different if Adam and Eve had not sinned? Why do you think they believed a snake instead of God?
- Why do you think God gave Adam and Eve the choice to obey or to sin in the first place?
- Adam and Eve suffered for their sins and people today are still paying the price. What are some ways you've paid for doing wrong?
- Think of something bad you're often tempted to do. What can you do to avoid giving in?

Go Deeper

Read John 8:42, 44; 14:21; Romans 5:12–21.

Prayer Starter

Ask God to help you choose to do the right thing when you're tempted.

Facts and Fun

No one knows what the Tree of Knowledge of Good and Evil looked like. Many people think it was an apple tree. Others think it was pomegranate. Draw a picture of what you think the Tree of Knowledge of Good and Evil and its fruit looked like.

Coming Up Next

Adam and Eve sinned, but it didn't stop with them. Next time, learn about two of their children and the trouble they got into!

WRONG!

Do you ever become upset and angry with your brothers or sisters? Probably most of us do. But what's the big rule? No *hitting*. Right? Read Genesis 4:1–16, 25–26 to find out what happened when one of Adam and Eve's sons became jealous of the other.

Think About It
- God looks at thoughts and attitudes. How would you describe Abel's attitude? Cain's?
- What are some things you can do to keep a positive, loving attitude toward your sisters and brothers when they really bug you? How do you think God wants you to respond?
- Are you like Cain in any way? Are you jealous of someone? Do you ever hold grudges or stay angry? What do you do when you're angry?

Go Deeper
Read Ephesians 3:16–21; Philippians 2:12–13; Hebrews 11:4; 1 John 3:11–12.

Prayer Starter
God can change your attitude. Tell Him about it when you're angry or upset or jealous. Ask Him to help you become an Abel, not a Cain.

Facts and Fun
What did Adam and Eve do when they were expelled from the Garden of Eden?
(Answer: They raised Cain.)

Coming Up Next
People laugh at a man who spends 120 years building a monstrous wooden "box." Learn next time about who has the last laugh!

ANGER/ATTITUDES/JEALOUSY

NOAH BUILDS A BIG BOAT

Everybody get on the Time Trampoline! We're going to take a huge leap forward in time from the days of Adam and Eve, and Cain and Abel. Now there are lots and lots of people in the world. Read Genesis 6:9–7:10 to find out why this is not necessarily good.

Think About It

- Imagine what it was like for Noah to build the ark day after day, year after year. What do you think about his problems, fears, and hopes?
- Noah walked with God. What do you think the words "walked with God" mean? What specific things can you do to please God?

Go Deeper

Read Philippians 1:9–11; 2:14–15; Hebrews 11:7; 1 Peter 3:18–21.

Prayer Starter

Ask God to help you be obedient like Noah. Talk to Him about big jobs—like cleaning your room or the yard—that you don't like.

Facts and Fun

Pretend that Noah could take another person on the ark, so he placed this ad in the newspaper.

MANURE MOVER WANTED
Must be good with a shovel, work in stinky conditions, and like animals.
Benefits: Will be saved from destruction.
Call 1–800–NOAH

Now write your own ad!

Coming Up Next

What would it be like if your ship was lost at sea in a terrible storm—and you couldn't see any land for months? Read about it . . . next time!

LARGE BOAT AFLOAT WITHOUT A RUDDER

Boring! Noah and his family were in the ark for 1 year and 17 days. What a long time to spend with a noisy, smelly zoo of animals! Read about it in Genesis 7:11–8:12.

Think About It

- How much work do you think it was feeding all those animals every day? How did the ark sound and smell?
- What are you waiting for that seems to take a long time? Can you trust God to take care of it?
- There was no way to steer the ark. Without a rudder, oars, sails, or a motor, Noah had no choice where he went. Things seemed totally out of control, but God was in control. Who is in control of your life?

Go Deeper

Read Genesis 8:13–19; Proverbs 3:5–6; Jeremiah 17:7–8; Luke 17:26–27.

Prayer Starter

God always answers prayer. His answers are "yes," "no," and "wait." Talk to God about what you're waiting for and how you would feel about it if His answer was "no" or "wait." Then pray for your family and friends.

Facts and Fun

Unscramble these words from Genesis 7:11–8:12.

kar   folod   nreva   lovie nabrch   vode

(Answers: ark, flood, raven, olive branch, and dove)

Coming Up Next

Do you "cross your heart" when you make a promise to show you really mean it? Next time, learn about God's colorful light show when He made a promise to Noah!

SIGNATURE IN THE SKY

What's the best part of a storm? As far as many people are concerned, the best part is when it's over! And the appearance of a rainbow is a special bonus. Read about the first rainbow and its special meaning in Genesis 8:20–9:17.

Think About It

- Covenants are contracts or very serious promises and are usually sealed and signed with a signature, stamp, or thumbprint. What was God's signature on His promise to Noah?
- Are you good at keeping your promises? Why or why not?
- God never breaks a promise He makes to you. How does knowing that make you feel?

Go Deeper

Read Deuteronomy 7:9; Isaiah 54:9–10; Romans 4:20–22.

Prayer Starter

Write a prayer to God telling Him how you feel about His promise of never again destroying the world with a flood. Thank Him for His promises.

Facts and Fun

Using crayons or paint, draw a rainbow. Or hold a piece of a chandelier (or some glass) in the sunlight and make rainbow colors on the wall.

Coming Up Next

How would you feel if all your friends forgot English and only spoke languages you couldn't understand? Next time, learn about some people who had that problem!

BABBLE, BABBLE, BABBLE

Did you ever notice how much most people talk? We talk to our families, friends, and our friends' friends. But these days we hear lots of people talking to each other in languages we can't understand. Where did all these languages come from? Read Genesis 11:1–9 to find out!

Think About It

- The people were thinking about how great they were, not about God. Why do you think this displeased God?
- What are some things you are good at? Even if you have a lot of natural abilities, you can't do everything. You still have to depend on God. How is this good?
- What talents do you have? How can you use them to please God?

Go Deeper

Read Genesis 11:10–26; John 8:50; James 4:10; 1 Peter 5:5–7.

Prayer Starter

Thank God for your abilities and ask for His help to use them wisely.

Facts and Fun

"Babel" sounds like the Hebrew word for "confused." The Tower of Babel was probably a ziggurat, a temple that looked like a pyramid which was used for worship. Most ziggurats had seven stories. Each story was slightly smaller than the one below it.

Coming Up Next

Did you ever have to pack all your belongings into a moving van and move away from your friends? Learn about someone who was told to move without knowing where he was going . . . next time!

YO, ABRAM, I NEED YOU!

Has your family ever moved? Usually many plans are made about how, when, and especially where to move. Read Genesis 12:1–9 to learn about a city boy from Ur hitting the road for an unknown destination.

Think About It
- God told Abram to go on a long journey. He also promised to bless him and make his descendants into a great nation. Imagine being in Abram's sandals. How would you have felt?
- How would you feel if tomorrow your family moved to a poor country halfway around the world?
- Sometimes obedience is tough, but look at the blessings Abram's obedience brought! Think of times you obeyed. What were the results?

Go Deeper
Read Genesis 11:27–32; 12:10–20; 1 Samuel 15:22; Isaiah 55:8–9; Acts 7:2–5; Hebrews 11:8–10.

Prayer Starter
Think of things your parents tell you that are difficult for you to obey. Ask God to help you be obedient.

Facts and Fun
Find a map of Bible lands in Abram's day. (There might be one in the back of your Bible.) With your finger trace Abram's journey. Remember, he went on foot and it took many weeks!

Coming Up Next
Have you ever argued with someone over who should get the bigger cookie or piece of cake? Next time, learn about two people who had to split something!

YOU TAKE IT.
NO, YOU TAKE IT!

Have you and someone else ever had to decide who gets something special? Did you think about it or just take what you wanted? Read Genesis 13:1–18 to find out how Abram and Lot faced a tough choice.

Think About It
- Abram let Lot choose first, and sure enough, Lot chose the best, most well-watered land. Did Abram lose out? Why or why not?
- Why is it hard to let others choose first? What is your biggest worry when others have first choice?
- How can you have Abram's attitude?

Go Deeper
Read Genesis 14:1–24; Philippians 2:4; Hebrews 13:16.

Prayer Starter
Genesis 13 begins and ends with Abram building an altar and worshipping God. Tomorrow, begin the day asking God to be with you and to help you be generous. End the day by thanking Him for the day and how He took care of you.

Facts and Fun
Before Josh went out to play, his mother reminded him, "Be sure to share your toys with your brother."

"Sure, Mom," Josh said. He thought a minute, then said to his brother, "I'll ride down the hill in the wagon, and you can pull it up the hill."

Coming Up Next
Have you ever been disappointed when you just couldn't have something you wanted? Learn how Abram felt, and what God did . . . next time!

PLEASE SIGN ON THE DOTTED LINE

When you feel sad or disappointed, what do you do? Do you go to someone for advice or comfort? Read Genesis 15:1–10, 17–21; 17:1–10 to find out how Abram was comforted.

Think About It

- God gave Abram great promises, but then Abram went years and years without receiving what God promised him. How would you feel if you were Abram?
- Think of times you need to feel safe and loved by God. How do you react to God's promise that He will be with you?
- What virtues did Abram have that you'd like?

Go Deeper

Read Genesis 15:11–16:14; 17:11–14; Joshua 1:9; Psalm 27:1; Romans 4:1–13.

Prayer Starter

Along with your other prayers, talk to God about times you need comfort or encouragement. Thank Him for His promise to be there for you.

Facts and Fun

Make a time capsule from a coffee can with a lid. You might put a baseball card and a newspaper clipping into it. You could also write a promise and stick it in. Bury the time capsule or hide it in your room. Forget about it until you discover it again! Has the promise come true?

Coming Up Next

Do you think God has a sense of humor? Do you think some very serious adults have a sense of humor? Next time, learn how God made an old woman named Sarah laugh!

NINETY-YEAR-OLD WOMAN GIVES BIRTH!

It's really hard to wait for a long time for something to happen. We become impatient and start thinking it will *never* happen. Read Genesis 18:1–15; 21:1–7 to find out how Abram, now called Abraham, and Sarah's long wait was rewarded.

Think About It
- Sarah laughed and then lied. Why?
- Think about a time when you laughed or said, "Oh, sure!" when someone promised to do something. How did you feel when they actually *did* it?
- God is bigger than any of our problems. Think of one of your problems. If God can give a very old woman a baby, what can He do for you?

Go Deeper
Read Genesis 21:8–20; Psalm 139; Jeremiah 32:17, 27; Romans 4:17–22; Hebrews 11:11–12.

Prayer Starter
You are not an accident. God has a plan for your life as He did for Isaac's. Thank God for your life, and ask Him to make you what He wants you to be.

Facts and Fun
The name Isaac means "laughter"; Abraham means "father of a multitude," and Sarah means "princess." What does your name mean? If you can't find out, write something that best describes you.

Coming Up Next
It's tragic when people are killed in earthquakes, hurricanes, or floods. Learn about two cities that caused their own disaster . . . next time!

NOW YOU SEE IT! NOW YOU DON'T!

How do you feel about friends or classmates who keep on doing wrong things? How do you act toward them? Read Genesis 18:20–32; 19:1–3, 15–29 to find out how Abraham felt about his wicked neighbors.

Think About It
- Abraham cared about the people in Sodom who were not wicked. How many people were rescued?
- God loves us but we still suffer for sin. Do you think God is fair for punishing sin? Why or why not?
- When other kids try to get you to do bad things, what can you do to not give in to peer pressure?

Go Deeper
Read Exodus 34:6–7; Psalm 86:15; Luke 17:28–30; 2 Peter 2:6–9.

Prayer Starter
If you know someone who is sinning, ask God to help him or her realize that what he or she is doing is wrong and ask for His forgiveness.

Facts and Fun
From the top of the mountain near Hebron, Abraham could see the Valley of Siddim and the wicked cities far below. And he could see the smoke of the burning cities. Lot was much closer, and he thought the world was ending!

Coming Up Next
Have you ever been faced with a really hard test? Next time, learn about Abraham's super big test!

TEST TODAY! UGH!

What if someone you loved and trusted asked you to do something you absolutely did not want to do? That's what happened to Abraham. Read Genesis 22:1–19 to get the story.

Think About It

- God had performed a miracle to give Isaac to Abraham and Sarah. Why do you think Abraham obeyed God now?
- After God provided the ram for the sacrifice, how do you think Abraham felt?
- What would you think if a stranger told you to cancel all your plans for next week? If your mom or God told you to? What's the difference?

Go Deeper

Read Genesis 24:1–67; 1 Samuel 15:22; John 14:23; Hebrews 11:17–19.

Prayer Starter

Ask God to help you obey His commands in the Bible even when it's tough and doing your own thing would be easier and more "fun."

Facts and Fun

The word "offering" today has a different meaning than it did in Old Testament times. Instead of putting money into a collection plate, the people placed an animal or food on an altar and burned it before the Lord. Burnt offerings were made to ask forgiveness for sins, to give thanks, or to praise God.

Coming Up Next

Have you ever had anyone offer to buy one of your favorite toys? Learn about a sneaky buyer and a careless seller . . . next time!

OBEDIENCE/TRUST

ALL MY BELONGINGS FOR SALE! CHEAP!

Have you ever given someone something you really should have kept—and then been sorry? Read Genesis 25:19–34; 27:6–16, 27–35 to find out about the most expensive bowl of stew ever!

Think About It
- In Genesis 27, Rebekah and Jacob lied to get the blessing. Think of other ways God could have had His word come true without them "helping" Him by sinning.
- When God wants something to happen, what can stop it?
- God knew you even before you were born. He has a great plan for your life. What can you do (for example, study hard at school) to "help" God's plan work out?

Go Deeper
Read Psalm 139:13–16; Jeremiah 29:11; Romans 9:10–13.

Prayer Starter
Think about how awesome it is that God knew you before you were born. Ask Him to show you what He wants you to do when you grow up.

Facts and Fun
In the Bible, the oldest son had the "birthright" to inherit most of the herds, flocks, and riches of his father. Isaac was like a millionaire! He had a "business" with over 300 employees. Yet Esau traded all that for a single bowl of lentil stew.

Coming Up Next
Do you ever feel like running away from your problems? Next time, learn about what happened to someone who did just that!

MAN SEES STAIRWAY TO HEAVEN

Did you ever have such a great dream that you didn't want to wake up? Read about a truly extraordinary dream in Genesis 28:10–22; 35:1–12.

Think About It
- Jacob was an ordinary person. Why do you think God chose such an ordinary person to do such an important job?
- Do you have to be perfect for God to use you? Why or why not?
- Jacob changed as he grew. How has God changed you as you've grown?

Go Deeper
Read Genesis 27:41–29:30; 1 Corinthians 15:10; 2 Timothy 2:20–21.

Prayer Starter
Start a prayer journal. Buy or make a blank book. Make four columns with these headings: Column 1—Date; Column 2—Prayer Request; Column 3—Date Answered (when God answers your prayer); Column 4—How Answered (brief explanation of how your prayer was answered).

Facts and Fun
Jacob had a dream of many angels in Bethel and said, "This is the house of God!" David had a vision of one angel in Jerusalem and said, "The house of God is to be here!" And the house of God was built in Jerusalem.

Coming Up Next
Have you ever seen huge sumo wrestlers on TV? Can you imagine a three-year-old boy against a 400-pound champion sumo wrestler? Stranger things have happened. Read all about it . . . next time!

WRESTLING MATCH TONIGHT

Have you ever been afraid of meeting up with someone who scares or worries you? Do you stay out of his way and sort of disappear when you see him coming? Jacob felt that way about Esau. Read Genesis 32:1–16, 23–31 for the story.

Think About It

- When it looked like Esau was coming with 400 men to attack him, Jacob reminded God that He had told him to come back to his family. Why do you think Jacob reminded God?
- God was far stronger than Jacob was. He could have won in a second. Obviously, He didn't use all His power. Why do you think God wrestled with Jacob?
- God could easily *make* you do things His way. Why doesn't He?

Go Deeper

Read Genesis 31:1–33:20; Matthew 19:26; Hebrews 2:8.

Prayer Starter

Find a promise God has made in the Bible, and next time you pray for something, remind God of His promise. (You'll find some promises in Psalms and John 13–17.)

Facts and Fun

What did Jacob have in common with Abraham, Sarah, Daniel, Peter, and Paul?
(Answer: They all changed their names.)

Coming Up Next

Think of the greatest piece of clothing you have ever had. What was special about it? Next time, learn about a special coat that caused serious trouble!

HE BUGS ME

Do you have a brother or sister who really bugs you? Does he or she seem to purposely do things that annoy you? Read Genesis 37:2–11, 18–28 to learn about a whole group of brothers who felt that way.

Think About It
- How could Joseph's brothers have handled their feelings differently?
- What could Joseph have done not to aggravate or bug them?
- Who or what makes you jealous? What can you do to control your anger and jealousy?
- Is someone jealous of you? What might you be doing to make things worse? What could you do to help them not be jealous?

Go Deeper
Read Genesis 39:1–40:23; Proverbs 14:30; 1 Corinthians 13:4; Titus 3:3–8.

Prayer Starter
Think of things that make you jealous. Ask God for forgiveness and for help to see things His way.

Facts and Fun
Why get so mad about a robe? Joseph's robe was long-sleeved and brightly colored—a sign that he was Jacob's favorite son. Wearing this robe probably excused Joseph from jobs that might have caused the robe to become dirty or ripped.

Coming Up Next
Have you ever had a horrible day when you thought things couldn't get any worse—and then they did get worse? Next time, learn about how Joseph's day went from bad to really awful.

ANGER/JEALOUSY

SAY WHAT?

Think of your most horrible, rotten day, when you didn't deserve what happened to you and it wasn't your fault. Read Genesis 39:1, 20–23; 41:14–40 to find out about Joseph's mega-bad day, month, and years.

Think About It
- Joseph didn't deserve what happened to him, but he didn't get angry or bitter. How did God use his bad situation to bless Joseph?
- Think of times you've been treated unfairly. How did it make you feel?
- It took a long time, but God blessed Joseph. What can help you stay true to God when you are treated unfairly?

Go Deeper
Read Genesis 47:13–27; 50:15–26; Psalm 105:16–22; Jeremiah 31:3; Acts 7:9–10; 1 Peter 5:10.

Prayer Starter
Thank God for always being with you even in tough times. Ask Him to be with others you know who really need His help or comfort.

Facts and Fun
In Bible times, kings and rulers always wanted to know what their dreams meant. The ancient Egyptians had entire books explaining how to interpret dreams and they *still* couldn't interpret Pharaoh's dream. Yet with God's help, Joseph did.

Coming Up Next
When someone treats you unfairly, do you feel like getting even? Learn how Joseph treated his brothers when *he* had a chance to get even . . . next time!

FAMILY REUNION

How do you feel about family reunions? Do you think they are fun or boring? Read Genesis 42:1–6; 45:1–11; 46:1–4; 50:15–21 to find out about a reunion to end all reunions.

Think About It
- How do you think Jacob's sons felt when they realized that their brother, Joseph, was a very important official in Egypt?
- Joseph forgave his brothers, knowing that God turned their sin into good. On a scale of 1–10, where "1" stands for "very hard" and "10" stands for "very easy," how easy do you find it to forgive people who hurt you?
- In a hopeless situation, how can you stay faithful like Joseph?

Go Deeper
Read Luke 17:3; Acts 7:11–15.

Prayer Starter
If there is someone you need to forgive, ask God to help you. If you feel your situation is hopeless, ask God for help.

Facts and Fun
Have you ever seen a picture of a mummy? When Egyptian pharaohs died, they were "embalmed"—wrapped in strips of linen. Joseph was an important Egyptian official, and when he died, they made him into a mummy, too.

Coming Up Next
Newborn babies are pretty helpless and need protection. Next time, learn about one baby who went for a wild river ride!

EXODUS-DEUTERONOMY

Tie on your sandals, grab your walking stick, and prepare for a fantastic journey with the special people of God, the Israelites. Be glad you're young because this journey takes more than 40 years! Before the journey begins, the Israelites are in big trouble. They are slaves in Egypt, but God saves them! God sends Moses to lead the Israelites, and He makes Pharaoh let them go.

Come along and walk through a sea on dry land, and get special food from God and water from a rock. Hear God speak from the top of a smoking, shaking mountain as He tells the people how to love and obey Him. Help build a special place of worship, and praise God there. See a golden calf, a bronze snake on a pole, and meet a talking donkey. Witness how the Israelites disobeyed God and were made to wander in the desert for 40 years. In spite of the Israelites' stubbornness, learn how God always showed His love to them even when they whined and disobeyed.

Who Wrote These Books

Moses wrote these four books, as he did Genesis. They are called the *Pentateuch*, which means "five books." Exodus, Leviticus, Numbers, and Deuteronomy were probably written between 1440 and 1400 B.C. This covered the time the Israelites wandered in the wilderness until they were ready to enter Canaan.

Why These Books Were Written

Exodus reminds the Israelites how God rescued them and formed them as a nation. The giving of the Law is also found in Exodus. In Leviticus God gives the Israelites instructions on how to live with each other and with Him. Numbers tells about the Israelites' 40 years in the desert to show God's judgement, but it also shows His faithfulness, love, and patience with His chosen people. Deuteronomy records Moses' final words to the Israelites before they entered the Promised Land—it was his challenge to obey God faithfully.

The overall message of these four books is first, that God is faithful, loving, merciful, forgiving, and patient; and second, that when we do things God's way, things go well, but when we choose our own way, things go badly.

FROM BULRUSH BABY TO PALACE PRINCE TO CONVICTED KILLER

If your country's leader ordered you to do something, you should do it, right? What might happen if you broke a law you thought was wrong? Read Exodus 1:8–2:10 to discover what some women did.

Think About It
- Think of a time you were told to do something you knew was wrong. What did you do? Was it hard to decide what to do? Why or why not?
- What do you think makes something right or wrong? Who decides?
- When your friends are all doing something, how do you know whether or not it's right for you to do it, too?

Go Deeper
Read Psalm 40:8; Matthew 7:21; Acts 7:17–29; Hebrews 11:23–27.

Prayer Starter
God knows everything and wants to hear about all your concerns and thoughts. When you're asked to do wrong, talk to God about your feelings. Tell Him about those hard decisions, and then ask for help to know what to do.

Facts and Fun
The name Moses means "is born" in Egyptian. Moses also sounds like the Hebrew word for "draw out." This emphasizes how God saved baby Moses by having him drawn out of the water.

Coming Up Next
Did you ever see a fire that burned with no fuel at all? Learn about this amazing happening . . . next time!

MYSTERIOUS DESERT BLAZE

Moses had been an Egyptian prince but now he was a shepherd in the desert. Quite a change! Things might have been dull and boring, but they got a lot less boring when a special visitor came calling! Read about it in Exodus 2:23–3:15.

Think About It

- How do you act when you have to do a chore that seems way too hard? Do you ask for help? Whom do you ask?
- How do you think Moses felt? How would you feel if God asked you to do the same thing today—and you *had* to succeed?
- What difficult thing (such as apologizing to a friend, understanding math, etc.) do you need God's help with?

Go Deeper

Read Exodus 3:1–5:23; Matthew 19:26; 22:31–32; Luke 1:37; Acts 7:30–35.

Prayer Starter

Think of some things that seem impossible for you. Talk to God about them and ask for His help. Remember that nothing is impossible for God.

Facts and Fun

What did the scared sheep at the burning bush say about Moses' answer to God?

(Answer: He's even more sheepish than I am!)

Coming Up Next

How would you like to live where the water is bloody, frogs are in your bed, and creepy crawly critters are everywhere? Next time, you can learn all about this "wonderful" place!

EGYPTIANS PLAGUED BY HORRORS

When Moses first appeared before Pharaoh, Pharaoh definitely thought he was in control, but soon he found out otherwise! Find out what caused this change by reading Exodus 7:15–18; 8:1–4, 16–17, 20–22.

Think About It
- Imagine you were a Hebrew slave in Egypt when the plagues struck. How would you feel? What would you see?
- When bad things are happening around you, how will it help you to realize that God knows what's going on and He is always in control?

Go Deeper
Read Exodus 7:13–10:29; Psalm 24:1; Romans 9:1; 1 Timothy 6:15.

Prayer Starter
There are people in the world today who have a life as tough as the Hebrew slaves had. Pray for God to help them.

Facts and Fun
Many of the plagues were directed against the "gods" of Egypt. An Egyptian goddess looked like a frog; the Egyptians worshiped many animals. Darkness was an insult to the sun god Ra.

Coming Up Next
Isn't that odd! All the dads in the neighborhood are out in front of their houses, painting their doorposts red. Find out why . . . next time!

GOD KEEPS HIS PROMISES

How would you feel if your dad told you, "Don't anyone step outside the house tonight. Bad things are happening! And get your shoes on! We're going to eat supper, then make a run for it"? What's happening? Read about this event, called the *Passover*, in Exodus 11:1; 12:1–13, 28–30.

Think About It

- God promised the Israelites that they would be safe if they obeyed Him. What rules do you need to keep—at home or on the playground—to keep you safe?
- Which promise do you think is harder for God to keep: freeing the Hebrews or His promises to love and protect and provide for you?

Go Deeper

Read Genesis 15:13–14; John 1:29; 1 Corinthians 5:7–8; 1 Peter 1:18–19.

Prayer Starter

Thank God for protecting you and your family, providing for you, and giving you rules to live by.

Facts and Fun

Jesus died for everyone's sins at Passover, the same day that Israelites in Egypt had killed a lamb and marked the doors so the angel of death would "pass over" their homes. That's why Jesus is sometimes called the "Passover Lamb."

Coming Up Next

An overnight flight is called a "red eye" because everyone is so sleepy, probably having red eyes from being unable to sleep. Next time, read about the biggest, most confusing, exciting "red eye" flight in history!

MILLIONS MARCH OUT OF EGYPT

It's dark outside and way, way past their bedtime, but thousands of children are in the streets, all leaving home at once—along with their moms, dads, sheep, cattle . . . Well, just read about it in Exodus 12:31–42.

Think About It
- Imagine you are in that midnight march with millions of people and animals. Imagine the noise and the confusion. What would you hear and see?
- Following instructions was very important during the Exodus (Israelites' mass exit from Egypt)! Can you think of times when it was important for you to follow instructions?
- The Israelites trusted God to care for them as they left Egypt. Whom do you trust? Why?

Go Deeper
Read Exodus 13:17–22; Psalm 105:36–39; Proverbs 16:20.

Prayer Starter
Thank God that you can always trust Him, especially during crazy times. Ask for help to follow His instructions.

Facts and Fun
The number of people leaving Egypt was about three million. That's more than the whole population of the city of Chicago marching out of Illinois! What a jam-up that would be on the highway!

Coming Up Next
Moses has a problem. He needs to get millions of people across the sea, but hardly anyone can swim and they have no boats. What now, Moses? Find out . . . next time.

WINDBLOWN WATERS AND WIPED OUT WARRIORS!

Could you swim across a large lake? What if someone was chasing you? This was the exact situation the Israelites were in. To find out how things turned out, read Exodus 14:9–31.

Think About It
- Try to imagine the rumbling of Pharaoh's chariots, and all the little kids crying as the Israelites are trapped by the sea. How would *you* be feeling?
- Holding back the Red Sea was a real miracle! What situations in your life do you need God to do a miracle in?

Go Deeper
Read Exodus 14:1–15:20; Psalm 91:14; John 14:14; 1 Corinthians10:1–2.

Prayer Starter
Thank God for helping you through tough situations in the past and for being so powerful. He can solve any problem.

Facts and Fun
A teacher told his students the parting of the Red Sea wasn't a miracle because the water was only three feet deep.

"That would have been even more of a miracle!" a student said.

"How so?" the teacher demanded.

"It would take some doing to drown the Egyptian army in three feet of water!"

Coming Up Next
How would you like to eat exactly the same food every day, and have to scrape it off the ground every morning? Next time, learn how the Israelites felt about their meals!

WILDERNESS WHINING

Imagine you are walking through a desert with very little food—and no McDonald's within hundreds of miles. What's your survival plan? Read Exodus 16:1–21 to discover what the hungry Israelites were doing.

Think About It

- How would you feel if your chore every morning, year after year, was to scrape a couple of gallons of manna off the desert rocks?
- How do you deal with being disappointed, frustrated, or bored silly? What makes you feel better? What happens when you trust God when you're in one of these moods?

Go Deeper

Read Exodus 15:22–17:7; Psalm 78:23–25; John 6:29–35.

Prayer Starter

Draw a circle with down-curving lines on the top and bottom and two eyes in the middle. You have a grouchy face—BUT turn it over and it's a smiley face. Look at "grouchy" and tell God what makes you grouchy. Turn the face around, tell God you've decided to be happy, and thank Him for helping you.

Facts and Fun

The word *manna* may mean "What is it?" or "Is it food?" It was white like coriander seed and tasted like wafers made with honey (Exodus 16:31) or something made with olive oil (Numbers 11:7–8).

Coming Up Next

Did you ever wish you could see God—even for one minute? Next time, learn what happened when God showed up!

FIRE, SMOKE, AND THE VOICE OF GOD

What is the most awesome thing you've ever seen? How did it grab your attention? Learn about one of the most awesome, attention-getting events that ever took place by reading Exodus 19:1–25.

Think About It

- If God appeared to you personally, what would you ask Him? What would you tell Him?
- You can't see God in person and hear Him talk out loud, but He answers your questions and tells you how to live through the Bible. The Bible is God's Word to us. Do you have any favorite Bible stories?
- How can reading the Bible make you a stronger Christian?

Go Deeper

Read John 5:39; 2 Timothy 3:15–17; Hebrews 1:1–2; 12:18–29.

Prayer Starter

God speaks to you through the Bible and people who teach you about Him. Thank God for talking to you, and ask for His help in understanding what He's saying.

Facts and Fun

There are 66 books in the Bible with a total of 1,189 chapters and 31,173 verses, containing 773,746 words and 3,566,480 letters. The longest verse is Esther 8:9 and the shortest is John 11:35. (Based on King James Version.)

Coming Up Next

How do you feel when you are handed a list of rules? Learn how the Israelites reacted . . . next time!

TOP TEN RULES

Remember a time when you went into a new classroom? Were you given a list of rules? Do you think rules are necessary? Read Exodus 20:1–17; 24:12–18 to find out how God feels about rules.

Think About It

- The first four commandments tell us how to have a good relationship with God. Commandments five to ten tell us how to get along with other people. Do you think one of these sections is more important than the other? Why or why not?
- Which of the Ten Commandments are the most difficult for you to obey? Why? What good can you see coming out of obeying these commandments?

Go Deeper

Read Exodus 22:20–24:3; Matthew 22:37–39; Romans 13:10; James 2:8–11.

Prayer Starter

Thank God for giving you the Ten Commandments for a good life, great friendships, and happiness. Ask for God's help to obey them.

Facts and Fun

God gave Moses the Ten Commandments in a special way. Find out what that was by reading Exodus 31:18 and Deuteronomy 9:10. Pretty awesome, isn't it?

Coming Up Next

If you were asked to help build a place of worship that met the needs of three million, what could you do? Next time, learn about someone who was asked that very question and find out how he answered!

TALENT SHOW

Think of people you know. What things can they do really well? Playing basketball, making people laugh, or wiggling their ears might be some of their talents. Read about some Bible-time talented people in Exodus 31:1–11; 37:1–9.

Think About It
- God gives everyone at least one talent and sometimes several. What talents has God given you? How are you using and developing them?
- How much do you think God enjoyed the results of Bezalel's work? How might He feel when you use the talents He has given you?

Go Deeper
Read Exodus 25:1–22; Deuteronomy 10:3–5; 2 Chronicles 35:3; Hebrews 9:3–5.

Prayer Starter
Thank God for the talents He has given you. Then ask for His help in developing them, for time to practice them, and for a way to help or entertain others.

Facts and Fun
The ark of the covenant contained the tablets of the Law (the covenant), Aaron's rod, and a pot of manna that never rotted! Two gold angels, called cherubim, were made and placed on its top. It was kept in the most holy place, in the Tent of Meeting, as a reminder of God's presence.

Coming Up Next
Something golden and shiny made the Israelites act in a very stupid way. Learn about their weird behavior . . . next time!

WORTHLESS WORSHIP

The Israelites had experienced awesome things—miracles, God's voice, and daily manna. But they were fickle followers! Read Exodus 32:1–20, 30–35 to find out what they did.

Think About It
- You might have idols too. Idols can be things you spend most of your money and time on that you think can make you happy. What idols might you have in your life?
- Compare those idols to God's love and care for you, His knowledge of your needs, and His ability to help you. Who comes out on top?

Go Deeper
Read Deuteronomy 9:7–21; Psalm 106:19–23; Luke 4:8; 1 Corinthians 10:6–8.

Prayer Starter
Obeying the first commandment can be hard because there are many things that want your attention, time, and money. Honestly talk to God about things you're tempted to value more than Him. Thank Him for being loving and forgiving, and ask for help to put Him first.

Facts and Fun
The golden calf was probably similar to idols the Egyptians worshiped. Aaron mistakenly thought it would represent God, which is why he declared a "festival to the LORD" (Exodus 32:5). Dumb move, Aaron.

Coming Up Next
Have you ever heard of people who were so embarrassed they wanted to cover their heads? Next time, learn how Moses needed to hide his face!

THE GLOWING FACE

Have you ever met someone who spent so much time with God that his or her face seemed to glow with His joy and peace? Read Exodus 34:1–11, 28–35 to find out how the Israelites ran away from someone like that.

Think About It
- Moses had broken the first two stone tablets. Now God gave him and the Israelites another chance. How do you think Moses felt?
- A person's character is what they are like, how they act. What do God's actions here tell you about His character?
- How can others see that you are God's child?

Go Deeper
Read Exodus 33; Leviticus 11:45; Numbers 14:17–20; 2 Corinthians 3:7–18.

Prayer Starter
Make a list of your good characteristics (you're kind, loving, etc.) and a list of your not-so-good characteristics (you cheat, fight, etc.). Thank God for your good characteristics and pray for His help in getting rid of the bad ones.

Facts and Fun
Moses wasn't the only person in the Bible who had a glowing face. When Jesus was with His disciples on the mountain where the Transfiguration took place, His face "shone like the sun" (Matthew 17:2).

Coming Up Next
Do you ever say, "What can I do? I'm just a kid!"? Learn about how everyone did *something* to help out . . . next time.

BECOMING LIKE GOD AND JESUS

WORSHIPING GOD WITH HAMMERS, CHISELS, AND NEEDLES

Does your church have a "Prayer Room" where people can pray and focus on God? What if it was a tent filled with gold in the desert? Read Exodus 36:1–6; 38:1–7; 40:1–8, 33–38 to find out about just such a place of worship.

Think About It
- If you knew God would show up in your church in a cloud of glory, how might the worship service be different?
- The Israelites saw God's presence. But you don't need to see God for Him to be with you. How else can you tell He is with you?

Go Deeper
Read Exodus 26:1–37; Psalm 100:2; Mark 12:30; Hebrews 9:1–8.

Prayer Starter
Worship God outside today. Find a quiet spot and along with your other prayers, use a praise prayer from the Bible such as Psalm 98 or Luke 1:46–55.

Facts and Fun
Have you ever heard a pastor say, "Stop giving! We have too much money!"? That's what Moses told the Israelites. Where did a bunch of slaves get so much for the tabernacle in the middle of the wilderness? They were gifts from the Egyptians! (Exodus 12:35–36).

Coming Up Next
How would you react if you had been treated terribly for many years and suddenly were freed? Next time, you will be shocked to learn how some people reacted!

WE MISS BEING SLAVES!

Imagine that your family had been prisoners all the way back to your great-great-grandparents. And now you're free! Most people would *never* want to go back to such a horrible life when they're finally in a better situation. But read Numbers 11:1–20, 31–34 to find out some people who *did!*

Think About It

- How do you react when things go wrong or you don't get what you want? Like the Israelites (complaining) or like Moses (praying)? What complaints do you have right now?
- When you put God in charge of your life, you trust Him to take care of things, and you're thankful for what He does. How hard is it for you to let God be in charge?

Go Deeper

Read Psalm 78:26–31; Proverbs 3:5–6; 1 Corinthians 10:6, 11; 1 Peter 4:19.

Prayer Starter

Write your "wails" on a sheet of paper and then talk to God about each one. Tell Him exactly how you feel and ask for His help. Then crunch up the paper and throw it away.

Facts and Fun

"Knock! Knock!"
"Who's there?"
"Manna."
"Manna who?"
"Manna wish we had something else to eat!"

Coming Up Next

Did you ever want to be a spy on a dangerous mission? Learn about men who got that opportunity . . . next time!

TEN SCARED SPIES

Finally, they'd arrived at Canaan, the land God had promised to Abraham hundreds of years earlier. But they needed to know what this country was like. How were they going to find out? What would they do with the information? Numbers 13:1–3, 25–33; 14:1–8, 26–34 answer these questions.

Think About It

- Ten spies gave a fearful report and only two said God would help them. Why do you think the Israelites believed the ten spies instead of the two, Caleb and Joshua?
- If the Israelites had believed God's promises, they would have had courage. Have you ever thought about a Bible verse when you needed help or were afraid? How would it help you?

Go Deeper

Read Psalm 23; Isaiah 12:1–2; Hebrews 3:17–4:11.

Prayer Starter

Tell God about your fears and worries. Then if you haven't already, read Psalm 23 and thank God for wanting only good things for you.

Facts and Fun

Be a spy today. Pretend you and your friends are going to invade a mall. What report would you give your friends? What would they get as a result of invading? What problems would they face?

Coming Up Next

Have you ever been so thirsty you couldn't even spit? Next time, learn about a whole crowd of "spitless" people!

ROCKY WATER

The Israelites did a lot of complaining, and their grumbling finally got to Moses. Did he scream at them or hide in his tent? Did he ride off on his camel and leave them in the desert? Find out how Moses reacted to their whining by reading Exodus 17:1–7 and Numbers 20:1–13.

Think About It

- Imagine you're Moses and three million people walk up to you in the desert and say, "We're thirsty." What would you do?
- Just like Moses, you can ask for God's advice through prayer. Then what do you need to do with it?
- Why might Moses have thought *talking* to a rock would not do the trick?

Go Deeper

Read Deuteronomy 32:48–52; Psalm 106:32–33; Matthew 6:33; 1 Corinthians 10:1–4.

Prayer Starter

Copy Psalm 105:3 on a large piece of paper in big letters. Put the poster where you will see it every day. Think about the words as you pray to God for wisdom.

Facts and Fun

Why was Moses the first "rock and roll" star?
(Answer: He struck the rock and water rolled out.)

Coming Up Next

Did you ever have a nightmare about snakes? Learn how such a nightmare became a reality . . . next time!

SNAKE HEALER

Once again, the Israelites were grumbling and complaining instead of trusting God. This time, God became very angry with them! Had He finally had enough? Was this the end? Find out by reading Numbers 21:4–9. Then read John 3:14–17.

Think About It
- Imagine you just got bitten by a venomous viper and there's no medicine or doctor to help! What would you do?
- How does whining and complaining about things show that you don't completely trust God?
- When you are sorry for the things you've done wrong, what is God's reaction?

Go Deeper
Read Exodus 34:6; Numbers 21:10–35; 1 Corinthians 10:9–11; Ephesians 2:4–6.

Prayer Starter
Think of some of the ways you have disobeyed God. Talk to God about those times and ask for His forgiveness.

Facts and Fun
Imagine taking a walk through a hot, sandy wilderness. Not only are you tired, sweaty, and thirsty, but you also need to be on a constant lookout for the ankle biters! The Sinai desert is full of venomous snakes. A bite by a poisonous snake often meant a slow death with terrible suffering.

Coming Up Next
Have you ever wished you could carry on a conversation with an animal? Next time, learn about someone who did just that!

GUESS WHO'S TALKING!

The Moabites in the land of Canaan had heard about the great things God had done for the Israelites—and now the Israelites were ready to come into their land! Read Numbers 22:1–7, 21–38 to find out what happened.

Think About It
- Balaam heard from God, but he also wanted to get rich! Have you ever wanted something so much you were tempted to do wrong things to get it?
- Which is easier for God—to make a donkey talk or to help you understand His commands in the Bible? Why?

Go Deeper
Read Numbers 31:14–16; Joshua 13:22; Psalm 25:4–5; Isaiah 58:11; 2 Peter 2:15–16.

Prayer Starter
Read Psalm 25:1–10. Think about how God shows you what to do. Thank God for this and ask for help to follow Him.

Facts and Fun
Balaam talked with God, heard from God, and gave true prophecies. But he had some problems: he was proud of his gift, and even worse, he loved money and was willing to sin to get rich. Balaam's sins hurt God's people and cost him his life. What a bad example!

Coming Up Next
What would you do if an expert guide, leading you through a rugged wilderness suddenly disappeared? Next time, find out what the Israelites did when that happened to them.

LET'S GIVE A BIG WELCOME TO . . . JOSHUA!

Did you ever wonder if a new teacher would know what to do or wish the "old" person had stayed? People in the Bible felt that way too. Read about it in Numbers 27:12–23.

Think About It

- God chose Joshua to replace Moses because Joshua was obedient and full of faith. Why are these qualities important to God?
- Joshua had great relationships with God and Moses. How would that help him in his new job? Who do you have great relationships with? How do those relationships help you?

Go Deeper

Read Deuteronomy 34:1–Joshua 1:18; Matthew 19:19; John 8:31.

Prayer Starter

Print RELATIONSHIPS across the top of a paper and the names of people you have good relationships with under it. How is each person like Joshua? Thank God for making each person important in your life.

Facts and Fun

Samuel: "I think Moses is getting old."
Joseph: "What makes you think so?"
Samuel: "It takes him more time to rest up than it does to get tired."

Coming Up Next

If someone gave your family a huge estate with houses, gardens, pools, and playing fields, how would you feel toward that person? Next time, find out how God wanted the Israelites to thank Him.

LOVE THE LORD!

How do you let your parents know that you love them? How about your friends—how do you let them know that they are special? Read Deuteronomy 6:1–25 for some good ideas on showing love.

Think About It

- Stop and think about some of the things God has done for you and your family. What are they? What can you do to show that you're thankful?
- God provides a place for us to live, food, and all that we need. What else (such as friends or wisdom) does He provide? How can you thank Him?

Go Deeper

Read Deuteronomy 8:1–20; 28:1–14; Matthew 22:35–40; John 14:23; 1 John 4:19.

Prayer Starter

Think of some toys or clothes or other things you really like—or a fun outing you've had—and thank God for those things.

Facts and Fun

"Knock! Knock!"
"Who's there?"
"Sam."
"Sam who?"
"Sam times I think you don't love me like I love you."

Coming Up Next

Did you ever play a game where the coach told your team to stomp the other team mercilessly? Next time, find out God's "game plan" for the children of Israel!

LOVE GOD/OBEDIENCE

SEARCH AND DESTROY

Does it seem that everyone and everything wants you to make a choice? Each TV ad wants you to choose its cereal, or jeans, or CD. Do you find it hard to make choices? The Israelites had to make one of the most important choices ever. Read about it in Deuteronomy 7:1–21.

Think About It
- Think about the friends you hang out with. Who influences the other the most, you or them? How do you think God feels about that?
- God didn't want the Israelites to marry or be friends with certain people. Why was that? Are there certain people that you shouldn't be around? Why?

Go Deeper
Read Deuteronomy 9:1–6; Judges 2:1–3; Proverbs 18:24; 2 Corinthians 6:14–18.

Prayer Starter
Pray for your friends, mentioning them by name. Ask God to give you the kind of relationship with them that He wants.

Facts and Fun
The Bible talks about the Israelites battling the Hittites, but archaeologists couldn't find a trace of the Hittites. For centuries archaeologists thought there were no such people. When they started excavating in Turkey, however, they dug up the Hittite's capital city, Hattusa. Hey! The Bible was *right!*

Coming Up Next
Bountiful land! Brave, beautiful ladies! Battles and miracles! Blowing rams' horns! Walls collapsing! Get ready for the book of Joshua!

JOSHUA

Be strong and courageous!" was God's command to
Joshua. God wanted a strong leader to take the
Israelites into the Promised Land, so He chose Moses'
right-hand man. Look for great things to happen as you
travel with the Israelites into the land of Canaan promised
to Abraham, Isaac, and Jacob. This book is about the battles
and adventures the Israelites had in taking over the land of
Canaan. You can make a narrow escape down a red rope out
of Rahab's window with the spies Joshua sent into Jericho,
the world's oldest city. Imagine carrying the ark as God
dried up the Jordan River so that the Israelites could cross.
Follow God's unusual battle plans that helped Joshua tum-
ble the 40-foot walls of the strong city of Jericho.

God's Promises

Joshua was a great general, a man of strong faith in God, and, scholars believe, the author of this book. Even today military teachers and colleges study Joshua's battle plans against Canaan. Like Moses, Joshua wanted his people to obey God. Notice as you read this book, that when the people obeyed God things went well for them. But when they didn't obey . . . well, read and see what happened. They had to learn some hard lessons, but God's presence was with Israel and that meant sure victory!

God's Power

The Lord did bring the people into Canaan as promised. They didn't always obey everything He commanded, but God continued to forgive them. Joshua divided the land among the twelve tribes of Israel. Near the end of his life, Joshua gathered all the people together. He reminded them how good God had been to them. Joshua told them that God had kept every promise and asked them to promise to serve only God. We can serve God too. And we know that He keeps every promise He makes.

SAVED BY A RED THREAD

In the Bible, God did miraculous things (like parting the Red Sea) that got people's attention for miles around and helped them believe in Him. Read Joshua 2:1–24; 6:22–23 to learn about a woman who believed in God and what she did as a result.

Think About It

- Pretend you're in Jericho talking about the Hebrew army coming. What would you be worried about? After He parted the Red Sea, what would you think of the Hebrew God?
- Rahab acted on her belief and was saved. What's one thing you believe about God? How can you act on it?

Go Deeper

Read Ephesians 1:7; Hebrews 11:31; James 2:24–26.

Prayer Starter

Rahab's people worshiped gods of stone that they could see but that could not help them. Rahab began to believe in God whom she could not see but who could help, because He had saved the Israelites. Tell God what you believe He can do.

Facts and Fun

On a piece of paper write every other letter to find the word missing in the sentence below. Add this sentence and pin it up where you can see it each day.

God brings _____ to all who believe in Him.

S O A T L P V R A X T W I M O D N

Coming Up Next

The army picked the worst possible time—the spring floods—to invade the Promised Land. Will they be swept away? Find out . . . next time.

FLOOD STOPPER

The Jordan River was swollen with flood water! No one in their right mind would try to cross those raging brown waters! Or would they? Read Joshua 3 to see crazy, faithful action.

Think About It

- God made a way for the Israelites by removing a huge obstacle, the flooded Jordan River. If He did that, how can He help solve your problems?
- The ark of the covenant represented God. Why do you think it was sent into the river first?
- Imagine you're the lead priest carrying the ark into the raging water. And oh, by the way, you can't swim—you spent your entire life in the desert. How would you feel?

Go Deeper

Read Joshua 4; 2 Samuel 22:33; Psalm 37:23–24; 66:5–6; Proverbs 11:5.

Prayer Starter

Tell God how you feel when it is hard to follow Him. Tell Him about obstacles that make it difficult. Remember, He can remove obstacles. Ask Him to go ahead of you and make a way for you to do what He asks.

Facts and Fun

Joshua stacked stones as a memorial to remember God's promise. Write out five things God has done for you. Find some stones and build a memorial marker in your yard or on your windowsill. Place your list in or under the marker.

Coming Up Next

Check out the Israelites' crazy marching orders . . . next time!

GOD'S MIRACLES/TRUST

VICTORY MARCH

Have you ever thought that adults' instructions were silly but obeyed anyway and things worked out? Read Joshua 6:1–25 to discover the strange orders God gave His people.

Think About It
- What do you think the Israelites thought about the crazy marching orders? What would the people of Jericho have thought of the silent marching day after day?
- Think of some things God asked you to do that you didn't understand. Did you obey? What happened?

Go Deeper
Read Deuteronomy 6:3; Psalm 44:5–8; John 14:23; 2 Corinthians 10:3–5; Hebrews 11:30.

Prayer Starter
Think of something in the Bible that you don't understand. Thank God that His Word is true, even if it doesn't always seem to make sense.

Facts and Fun
Two kids debated God's existance. The girl asked: "Do you see God?"
Boy: "No."
Girl: "Exactly. We cannot see God because He is not there."
The boy asked: "Can you see yourself in a mirror?"
Girl: "Yes."
Boy: "Do you see your bones?"
Girl: "No."
Boy: "I guess that must mean you don't have any!"

Coming Up Next
Ever feel tempted to take something that didn't seem to belong to anyone? Read next time about a man with "sticky fingers."

SIN IN THE CAMP

People often think that disobeying is no big deal. Has there ever been a time when you thought disobeying was cool or okay, but then you got caught? What happened? The Bible tells a story about a man who found out about disobedience really quickly. Read Joshua 7:1–26 to get the story.

Think About It

- How did Achan's sin affect the whole camp? How many men lost their lives because of Achan?
- Are there some cool things that you're tempted to steal or "borrow" without asking? How can you resist temptation?
- Has there been a time when you did something wrong and it affected someone else? What happened?

Go Deeper

Read Joshua 8; Psalm 90:8; Luke 8:17; Colossians 3:1–6; Hebrews 4:13. '

Prayer Starter

Ask God to show you things you do that hurt yourself and that hurt others. Ask Him how you can change your behavior. Achan died for his sins, but God sent Jesus to die for ours. Thank God for His forgiveness through Jesus Christ.

Facts and Fun

Where did the Israelites keep their money?
(Answer: In the banks of the Jordan.)

Coming Up Next

Ever wish the sun wouldn't set so you could stay outside several more hours? Next time, read about a man who got that wish.

THE LONGEST DAY IN HISTORY

How can moldy bread and worn-out shoes lead to a huge mistake? Read Joshua 9:1–9, 14–16; 10:1–15 to find out.

Think About It

- God told Israel to destroy all the nations of Canaan. How would stopping to ask God for wisdom have changed this story?
- Have you ever made a major decision without asking your parents' permission? Or without praying? What happened?
- God may not make the day longer for you, but what things *has* He done for you when you needed help?

Go Deeper

Read Joshua 9 and 1 Chronicles 10:13–14 to find out what Saul and the Israelites had in common. Read Proverbs 2:3–5; Acts 7:45; Romans 8:31; 1 Corinthians 1:25.

Prayer Starter

Do you have to make a decision? Besides asking for your parents' advice, pray for wisdom.

Facts and Fun

Measure time by using your body as a sundial. Stand on the sidewalk and have a friend draw your shadow. Come back a couple of hours later, stand on the same spot, and do the same thing. Repeat this several times and notice how much the sun moved in a day.

Coming Up Next

These days, judges sit in a courtroom and listen to lawyers argue. Most of the judges of Israel, however, led armies onto the battlefield! Learn about the judges of Israel . . . next time!

JUDGES

The Israelites settled in the land God had promised them, but the story did not end there. The book of Judges tells how, in the centuries that followed, the Israelites often made bad choices in not following God. They had not destroyed all the Canaanite nations as God had commanded. What do you think they did then? The people soon forgot the Lord's commands and married people who worshiped false gods, and they began to worship idols themselves! Now that they were farmers in Canaan, the Israelites had to plant crops and vineyards. They thought God was a God of the desert and knew nothing about growing crops or making it rain. The Israelites worshiped the Canaanite gods, asking for help with their farming.

God's Discipline

In order to teach the Israelites that He is the true God, He punished them by allowing their enemies to defeat them. But the people cried out to God for forgiveness, so He chose leaders, called judges, to rule over the people and remind them of His Law. Many of the judges were military leaders and became judges after they led their people to victory. Again and again the Israelites forgot to obey God and forgot that the false god could not protect them. Again and again God allowed their enemies to tear the country apart. The Israelite tribes were attacked from every side. The Philistines on the coast and desert tribes from across the Jordan River invaded the land. Every time the Israelites cried to God for help, He sent a new judge to remind them of His promises.

Amazing Leaders

There were twelve judges over Israel. Read about Deborah who was called "the mother of Israel," Gideon who won battles in amazing ways, and Samson who slew hundreds of Philistines. The judges were wise heroes, but it was God who won the battles they fought. Even though their people worshiped false gods, the judges were willing to fight the enemies of God. The last judge of Israel, Samuel, probably wrote the book of Judges to tell us about these judges who loved God and tried to turn the hearts of Israel back to Him. Travel with these men and women to learn how you too can make good choices in following God.

DISASTROUS DISOBEDIENCE

In the Bible God sent judges to help guide His people and deliver them from their enemies. Read Judges 2:6–3:4; 21:25 to learn how the people kept getting into trouble again and again.

Think About It
- If God rescued the Israelites even after they had sinned and worshiped other gods, what do you think He will do for you after you sin?
- Do you have a younger brother or sister—or a friend—who always seems to get into trouble? Do you help that person? What is your attitude toward him or her?

Go Deeper
Read Judges 3 to learn more about the judges. Read Deuteronomy 5:7–8; Psalm 106:34–43; 1 Corinthians 15:33; 1 John 1:9.

Prayer Starter
Think of something wrong that you do over and over. Tell God why you think you keep making the same mistake. Maybe like the Israelites, you want to do things your way and not God's. Ask God for help.

Facts and Fun
Which judge was so frightened that he was hiding food when God came to him? *(Answer: Gideon.)*
Which judge was famous for being left-handed? *(Answer: Ehud.)*
Which judge killed a lion with his bare hands? *(Answer: Samson.)*

Coming Up Next
He had an army of ten thousand men, but he refused to go to battle unless a lady went with him. Read about it . . . next time!

WIMP OR WARRIOR?

Can you think of a time you were scared to do something, but then someone big and strong went with you? Read Judges 4:1–24 to learn about a woman who went with a warrior when he was worried.

Think About It

- Barak was a strong warrior, but his faith was weak. Deborah was not a warrior, but she trusted God. When something hard has to be done, are you more like Deborah or Barak? In what ways?
- God used another woman, Jael, to help win the war. People sometimes think certain groups of people are weaker or helpless. What's wrong with this attitude? Why?

Go Deeper

Read Judges 3:7–31; Proverbs 3:3–6; 1 Thessalonians 5:14; Hebrews 10:24.

Prayer Starter

Think of a time when you needed someone else's help. Now think of a time when God used you to help others. Thank God for the special people He's given to help you. Ask Him for chances to encourage others to trust Him too.

Facts and Fun

Which judge covered the entire courtroom with one hand? *(Answer: Deborah. "She held court under the Palm of Deborah" (Judges 4:5).)*

Coming Up Next

Have you ever sneaked up on somebody and scared them? Next time, learn about some people who were literally scared to death!

A SWORD FOR THE LORD

In the Bible, God's battle plans sometimes were a lot different from man's. The results, however, were a lot greater. Read Judges 6:11–16, 33–40; 7:1–7, 16–22 to find out some strange weapons God told Gideon to use to fight the Midianites.

Think About It

- What might have happened if the Israelites had not followed God's directions to hide their torches? Would the Midianites have been caught off guard?
- Have you ever had to follow specific instructions to get a job done? What happened if you missed some steps or did them at the wrong time?

Go Deeper

Read Judges 8 to learn more about Gideon. Read 1 Samuel 14:1–7; Psalm 27:11; 2 Corinthians 12:9.

Prayer Starter

Sometimes, like Gideon, you may feel like you're up against gigantic odds. Even math or other homework can seem that way. Ask God to help you overcome these problems.

Facts and Fun

Can you believe it? An hour before the battle, Gideon was still too afraid to fight the Midianites. What finally encouraged him? A Midianite man had a dream that Gideon was a giant round loaf of bread that rolled down the hill and knocked down a Midianite tent!

Coming Up Next

Have you ever had a bad hair day? Well, next time learn about a man with a really bad haircut!

A JUDGE WITH A BAD HAIRCUT

Have you ever had a friend lead you into a trap where your enemies beat you up? Read Judges 13:1–5, 24; 16:4–6, 17–30 to find out about a guy who was really betrayed by a friend.

Think About It

- After his haircut, Samson was left pretty weak. How do you feel after you give in to temptation—strong and courageous or weak and scared? Why?
- Samson paid a big price for giving in to Delilah, but he asked for forgiveness and God still used him. Is there a temptation in your life that you have given in to—maybe you cheated on a test or teased a classmate? What can you do, with God's help, to change that situation?

Go Deeper

Read Judges 14–15; Micah 7:5–6; 1 Corinthians 10:13; James 1:13–15.

Prayer Starter

Tell God how you gave in to temptation. Ask for His help to make you stronger than Samson next time.

Facts and Fun

Make a comic strip telling the story of Samson. Cut pictures out of newspapers or magazines and glue them on paper, or draw your own pictures. Write words in speech balloons for conversations of characters in the story.

Coming Up Next

Next time read about two women who survived famine and death and crossed mountains to another country to start over.

RUTH

The book of Ruth takes place in that dark time when Israel disobeyed God and judges ruled the people. Everyone looked after himself and didn't care about anyone else. God had disciplined Israel by sending a famine. Pack your bags and follow Naomi and her family to find food. Don't unpack! Follow Ruth and Naomi to learn a beautiful story of love and loyalty.

True Friendship

During the famine, Naomi and her husband moved to Moab to look for food. When Naomi's husband and sons died, she wanted to go back to her people in Bethlehem after the famine ended. Naomi's daughter-in-law, Ruth, loved her very much and wanted to go with her, even though Ruth was a Moabite. Ruth told Naomi, "Where you go I will go, and where you stay I will stay. Your people will be my people, and your God will be my God." Ruth chose to leave the idols of her people and worship the true God.

After arriving in Bethlehem, Ruth and Naomi had no money, so Ruth set out to get food for them. The Law said that at harvesttime some grain must be left for the poor to gather. Boaz was a rich farmer and a relative of Naomi. He spotted the beautiful Ruth picking up leftover grain. Can you guess what happened? Boaz and Ruth fell in love and were married. They had a son, Obed, making Naomi the proudest grandmother in all of Bethlehem.

A Redeemer

The great judge and priest, Samuel, wrote the book of Ruth to show that even in the worst of times, God watches over those who trust Him and do what is right. Ruth became the great-grandmother of David, Israel's greatest king. Ruth's story is about a kinsman-redeemer. The Law stated if a person lost his land, a close relative (a "kinsman") could buy it back ("redeem" it). Boaz married Ruth so Naomi's husband's property would be hers again.

This story is a wonderful glimpse of our Kinsman-Redeemer, Jesus. He was born as a human so He could become our kinsman, or part of our family. He bought us back and redeemed, or freed, us from our sins to bring us back to God. The Bible says that those who believe in Him will be His bride.

LASTING FRIENDSHIPS

What makes a good friend? Have you ever had a friend who left his or her family just to come live with you? Read Ruth 1:1–8, 14–19; 2:1–3; 4:5–17 to meet such a friend.

Think About It
- Ruth was loyal to Naomi, which means she was devoted, sincere, and caring. Who has been a loyal friend to you? How have you been a loyal friend?
- How did Boaz show loyalty to his relatives?

Go Deeper
Read Deuteronomy 31:6; Ruth 2–3; Proverbs 18:24; Matthew 1:1, 5; 1 Corinthians 13:3–8.

Prayer Starter
God is a loyal friend. He said, "Never will I leave you" (Hebrews 13:5). Thank God for this. Tell Him how you feel about His friendship and how He sent Jesus to "buy you back" or redeem you.

Facts and Fun
God wants us to help the poor. He commanded landowners not to harvest the edges of their fields (Leviticus 19:9–10). Then poor people could gather or "glean" the leftover grain. You can give the poor your "leftover grain" too. When you empty your pockets, put the change in a special place. Later send it to a missionary or a group that helps the poor.

Coming Up Next
Have your parents ever accidentally forgotten you in church? Next time, read about a mom who left her little boy in church on purpose!

1 & 2 SAMUEL

The books of 1 and 2 Samuel take up the story of the Israelites where the book of Judges ended. Hold on to your seat as you read the story of one of the most exciting times in the history of Israel. It's the story of battles, fighting giants, good and bad kings, and strong friendships.

"We Want a King!"

First and Second Samuel were probably one book at first. We're not sure who wrote them. Samuel, Israel's last judge, might have written parts of 1 Samuel. Other later prophets probably finished it and wrote 2 Samuel. Samuel was also a great prophet and priest and military leader. As Samuel grew old, the Israelites wanted a king to lead them. They wanted to be like the other nations around them with kings to fight their battles. Samuel warned the people that a king would rule harshly and reminded them that God had always fought their enemies. Imagine the crowd as they shouted their demands for a king. God told Samuel to choose Saul as king. The book of 1 Samuel tells of the rise and fall of King Saul. Saul was disobedient and didn't follow all that God commanded. Saul's disobedience made God sad. Later He told Samuel to anoint David as king of Israel.

Israel's Hero

First Samuel also gives us one of the most famous stories in the Bible, the story of young David's triumph over Goliath. Can you imagine being a teenage boy and facing a giant over nine feet tall? David was a man after God's own heart. He was also a great military leader who led Israel in victory over their enemies. The people loved their new hero, but King Saul grew jealous and tried to kill David, forcing him to live in hiding.

Do you have a really good friend? David did. Jonathan, Saul's son, was David's closest friend. Follow them to find out what good friendship is all about.

A Good King

Second Samuel tells how David first became king of Judah, then all of Israel. It tells of his successes and his failures. Jerusalem would be called "The City of David" because David captured it from the Canaanites and made it his capital. David was a good king and leader, but his family life was far from perfect. Read to find out the problems and sins that destroyed his family. Learn from David the benefits of being truly sorry and asking God for forgiveness for your sins.

LEFT BEHIND!

Who do you love very much? How would you feel if you had to give up that person? Read 1 Samuel 1:1–28; 2:21 to learn about a mother who gave up her son for the Lord's service.

Think About It

- How difficult do you think it was for Hannah to give up Samuel? Name some things that you think would be hard to give up in your life.
- Was it worth it for Hannah to make such a sacrifice and give up her son? Why?

Go Deeper

Read 1 Samuel 2:1–26. To find out more about giving all to God, read Luke 18:18–25; 2 Corinthians 9:7.

Prayer Starter

Everything belongs to God. Talk to Him about some of the things He's given you that you want to hold on to. Ask Him to help you give up those things if He asks you to.

Facts and Fun

In the Bible names were really important. Try to match the names of Hannah, Eli, and Samuel to their correct meanings below.

1. "Jehovah is high"
2. "grace"
3. "asked of God".

(Answer: 1. Eli; 2. Hannah; 3. Samuel)

Coming Up Next

Has your pastor ever called and awakened you in the middle of the night to ask you to do a small errand? No? Well, next time, read about a kid who thought that was happening.

LISTENING PAYS OFF

Have you ever missed someone calling you because you weren't listening? What happened? Did you lose out on something special? Read 1 Samuel 3:1–4:1 to learn what God said to a boy who listened to His call.

Think About It
- Imagine you are Samuel and you hear a voice calling your name in the middle of the night. What would you think?
- When you need to know what to do, what book will help you find God's instructions?

Go Deeper
Read 1 Kings 19:11–13 to learn more about the voice of God. Read Psalm 29:4; 46:10; Isaiah 50:4; John 10:3–4.

Prayer Starter
God speaks to us in many ways. Sometimes He speaks through the Bible. At other times God speaks through someone else, like a parent or pastor. Sometimes the birds singing or the wind blowing tell us of God's love. Thank God for all the different ways He speaks to you.

Facts and Fun
Ever feel like you have too many jobs in your house? As he grew up, Samuel had many jobs. Which of these do you think Samuel had?

Priest   Milkman   Farmer   Prophet   Judge   King
(Answer: Priest, Prophet, Judge)

Coming Up Next
Next time, read about some foolish people who thought God was in a box! And then they lost the box!

GOD IN A BOX!

Things like the Bible and church point us to God, but they are not God. Are there things you put your trust in more than God? Read 1 Samuel 4:1–22 to find out what the Israelites trusted in.

Think About It
- Imagine you are the Benjamite who saw the battle lost, the ark taken. You run excitedly to Shiloh. What happens?
- The Israelites forgot that God is living and powerful. Have you ever forgotten that God was there to protect you? What did you do?

Go Deeper
Read Psalm 20:7; Isaiah 55:9; Colossians 3:2.

Prayer Starter
We often forget how powerful God is, and think He can't help us. Tell Him honestly the ways you put limits on Him. Ask Him to help you trust Him more.

Facts and Fun
Why were the Philistines so frightened of the Israelites? The Philistines, called the "sea peoples," had invaded Canaan, Syria, and many other countries. But they could never defeat Egypt. Wouldn't you be scared of the people whose God sent plagues on Egypt and drowned their chariots in the Red Sea?

Coming Up Next
Since the beginning, people have built idols out of stone and wood and called them gods. Find out what happens when God makes an idol bow down . . . next time!

AN IDOL FALLS FLAT

Think of a time you felt God was trying to teach you something. For example, did you ever lose something valuable? How did you respond? Read 1 Samuel 5:1–12; 6:1–13 to meet some people who learned a lesson from God.

Think About It

- The Israelites' greatest treasure, the ark, was stolen. Later God returned the ark. Imagine you are an Israelite and you see the ark returning. How would you feel?
- God showed the Philistines that He was greater than their god. Which things do you value (skateboard? Walkman?) that God is greater than?

Go Deeper

Read Exodus 20:3–4; 1 Samuel 6:14–7:2; Psalm 72:9; Acts 17:24–25; Romans 14:11.

Prayer Starter

Think about times you have taken God for granted. Take a minute to think about how God is greater than anyone or anything in the entire world. Ask God to help you worship Him as the one true God.

Facts and Fun

God made the idol of Dagon fall down twice before the ark, but the Philistines kept worshiping Dagon. So a few years later, God sent along Samson to knock the entire temple of Dagon to the ground.

Coming Up Next

Ever wonder what happens when God gets angry and there's some thunder handy? Next time, learn about a day when God got upset and turned up the volume!

GOD OF THUNDER

Disobedience can keep God from helping us. If you want God to help you overcome your problems, what should you do? Read 1 Samuel 7:3–17 to find out what happened when the Israelites were in this situation.

Think About It

- As soon as the Israelites gathered together and told God they were sorry, God gave them a great victory over the Philistines. Why did they have to make things right *first?*
- Have you ever had problems, but then you were sorry and made things right? What happened then?

Go Deeper

Read Deuteronomy 6:18–19; 2 Kings 7:5–7; Job 37:5; Psalm 18:40.

Prayer Starter

Ask God to bring to mind anyone you've hurt and need to make things right with. Pray that God will give you the courage and humility to apologize.

Facts and Fun

"Mom, I want to ask you a question," said Tom after his first Sunday school class. "The teacher was reading the Bible to us—all about the children of Israel crossing the Red Sea, the children of Israel battling the Philistines, and the children of Israel making sacrifices."

"Yes, the children of Israel did many great things," answered Mother.

"Well . . . didn't the grown-ups do anything?"

Coming Up Next

Have you ever wondered how someone becomes president or king? Find out next time how it happened in Israel.

KING CRAZY

Ever wished you could hide behind a bodyguard? The Israelites had fought a lot of battles. They were tired and wanted someone to fight their battles for them. They didn't want to trust God, so they wanted a king. Read 1 Samuel 8:1–22 to find out what happened.

Think About It
- It was not wrong to have a king. But it was wrong for the Israelites to want a king to fight their battles. Why?
- Which is easier, to have someone tell you what to do or to try to figure it out yourself? Why?

Go Deeper
Read Deuteronomy 17:14–20; 1 Samuel 12:12–25; Psalm 95:3; 1 Timothy 1:17.

Prayer Starter
Sometimes it is easier to have someone else solve our problems instead of waiting on God. Be honest with God about why it is hard to wait on Him to lead you. Ask Him to be King of your life and guide you in all you do.

Facts and Fun
Say these tongue twisters five times.

Crazy kings catapult kooky Canaanite kids.

Cranky Canaanites crush cunning kings.

Coming Up Next
Ever get invited to a surprise party and have cooking oil dumped on your head? No? Well, it happened to one guy in the Bible. Read about it . . . next time!

GOD IS KING

THE MAN FOR THE JOB

Saul went out looking for his father's donkeys, and ended up with something much more valuable! Read 1 Samuel 9:3–27; 10:1 to find out what the prophet told him!

Think About It

- Saul was totally not expecting to be made king. Have your parents ever suddenly announced a reward or outing you weren't expecting? How did you feel?
- Have you ever whined to get your way, then have it turn out bad? What should you have done instead?

Go Deeper

Read Exodus 16 about another time God gave the people of Israel what they wanted because He understood their struggles. Read 1 Samuel 10:2–11:15; Acts 13:1–22.

Prayer Starter

Sometimes God gives us what we want, even though it may not be best. Ask God to help you trust that He knows what's best.

Facts and Fun

True or False
1. In Bible times a king was elected by the people.
2. Sweet oil on Saul's head showed that God had chosen him as king.
3. Saul's friends posted signs saying "Saul for King" throughout the country.
4. The people shouted, "Down with the king!"
(Answers: 1. F; 2. T; 3. F; 4. F)

Coming Up Next

Find out next time why it is important to "tell the whole truth and nothing but the truth."

WORD-GAME LOSER

Do you know the expression "playing word games"?
That's when you use words to get what you want. Read
1 Samuel 15:1–26 to discover how Saul tried to get out of
trouble by playing word games.

Think About It
- God ordered Saul to kill all the flocks and herds, but
  Saul "had a better idea." Have you ever done things
  differently than you were told? What happened?
- Have you ever been tempted to tell a half-truth to get
  your way or avoid getting in trouble? What did you do?

Go Deeper
Read 1 Samuel 13:1–14; 15:27–35; Psalm 51:6–7; 120:2;
Proverbs 10:19.

Prayer Starter
Think of times you told a half-truth or avoided telling the
whole story. Talk to God about this. Ask for help to tell the
whole truth.

Facts and Fun
A boy was talking to his dad:
Boy: "Dad, how long is a million years to God?"
Dad: "It is but a second."
Boy: "Dad, how much is a million dollars to God?"
Dad: "Oh, just a penny."
Boy: "Do you think God could give me a penny?"
Dad: "Sure, but you will probably have to wait a second."

Coming Up Next
The prophet Samuel went on a secret mission, and he
made sure that King Saul didn't know what he was doing.
Next time, find out why!

LYING

FROM THE INSIDE OUT

Have you ever wished you were as tall or good-looking as someone else? Cheer up! What's inside a person is far more important than how they look. Read 1 Samuel 16:1–23 to see how God chose between Eliab and David.

Think About It
- How did Saul's servant describe David? What was David's most important quality? Which of David's qualities would you like to have?
- We're all different, and God has designed each of us for special tasks. What do you think God might have you do when you grow up?

Go Deeper
Read Psalm 78:70–71; 89:19–20; 139:23–24; Matthew 23:25–26.

Prayer Starter
What good attitudes and qualities do you have? Now think of your behavior on the outside—does it match the inside? Ask God to give you a pure heart like David.

Facts and Fun
In Bible times, a shepherd had special equipment for his job: a sling to shoot stones at wild animals; a small leather bag to carry stones for the sling; a strong club with flints in it to attack intruders; a staff, or long stick, to guide the sheep; and a pipe or harp to calm them.

Coming Up Next
Ever heard the expression "Don't send a boy to do a man's job"? Next time, learn how God used a boy to do a giant job!

GIANT KILLER

What do giants, lions, and bears have in common? David!
Read 1 Samuel 17:4–11, 23–51 to find out how teenage
David knew he could beat Goliath because God had helped
him kill wild animals.

Think About It

- David did not need Saul's armor to protect him. He
  trusted God instead. Name some things (such as your
  own skill, your big brother) that you don't really need
  if God wants you to do a big job.
- What big problems can you overcome if you have the
  faith that God is with you? (for example, doing well
  in sports, making friends)

Go Deeper

Read 2 Samuel 21:15–22 to learn how David killed more
giants. Read 1 Corinthians 1:27; Hebrews 13:6.

Prayer Starter

Think of some BIG jobs that need to be done. Pray that
God will give you the faith to tackle them, and help you
do them.

Facts and Fun

David's sling was probably made from a small leather
patch with two long straps. The shepherd placed a small
rock in the patch and swung the sling over his head.
Letting go of one of the straps sent the rock flying at more
than 60 miles an hour to hit a target 50 yards away.

Coming Up Next

Ever been jealous because someone had something you
wanted? Find out next time how jealousy can mess up a
friendship!

A FRIENDSHIP IS DAMAGED

Think of a time you wanted something and someone else got it. How did you feel? How did you treat that person? Read 1 Samuel 18:5–16; 19:1–10 to find out what happened when Saul became jealous of David.

Think About It

- How should Saul have felt about David's success? What happened to their friendship because of his jealousy?
- Are you jealous of someone because he or she does something better than you? How does your jealousy affect your relationship?
- How do you think God wants you to behave when your friends do well? Why?

Go Deeper

Read 1 Samuel 18:17–30; 19:11–20:42; Proverbs 14:30; Romans 12:15; Philippians 2:3; James 4:1–2.

Prayer Starter

Honestly tell God about friends or classmates you are jealous of. Tell Him what they have that you want. Ask Him to show you ways to love them and be happy with them when they do well.

Facts and Fun

David was Saul's personal musician. This is generally not a dangerous job, but David never knew when he was going to have to duck a spear. He probably prayed for protection before reporting for harp duty.

Coming Up Next

Have you ever been tempted to play around with witchcraft or talk to ghosts? Next time, meet someone who did!

SAUL TALKS TO A WITCH

Can you remember at time you needed advice but went to the wrong person. Read 1 Samuel 28:1–25; 31:1–13 to find out what happened when Saul asked a witch (called a "medium") to help him.

Think About It
- Saul went to the medium because God was no longer speaking to him. He could have gotten back on speaking terms with God by being sorry for his sins. Why didn't he?
- Have you ever desperately needed to talk to someone, but were ashamed to because you weren't friends anymore? What did you do? What *should* you have done?

Go Deeper
Read 1 Chronicles 10:13–14 to learn more about what happened when Saul talked to a medium. Read 2 Samuel 1:1–27; Psalm 1:1; 90:12; Proverbs 1:7.

Prayer Starter
Some people who aren't Christians believe there are "good witches," and that it is okay to talk to ghosts. Pray for God to protect you from these bad influences.

Facts and Fun
God was upset with Saul for going to a medium for guidance. Today some people look to fortune tellers, horoscopes and even psychic phone lines for the same thing. God wants us to trust Him, the accurate source for wisdom and guidance.

Coming Up Next
Two kings in one country? That is not good! Next time, read how that dangerous situation worked out.

DISOBEDIENCE/OTHER GODS

NO! *I'M* THE KING!

David knew he was supposed to be king over all Israel after Saul died. There was only one little problem, however. Saul's son, Ish-Bosheth, was now king. Read 2 Samuel 2:1–11; 5:1–5 to find out what David did.

Think About It

- David often went to God for guidance. How would this make him a good king?
- David could have gone to war against Ish-Bosheth to take over the kingdom. Instead, he waited patiently for God to give it to him. Have you ever had to wait patiently for something? How did things work out?

Go Deeper

Read 2 Samuel 3–4; 5:6–12; Psalm 23 to find out what God will do for you. Read Psalm 89:19–23; John 10:1–16; Acts 13:21–22.

Prayer Starter

If there are some things in your life you can hardly wait for, ask God to give you patience. Ask Him to help you trust Him to do things in His time.

Facts and Fun

"Knock! Knock!"
"Who's there?"
"Les Crown."
"Les Crown who?"
"Les Crown David! He'd make a good king!"

Coming Up Next

Have you ever heard the expression "They're so happy, they're dancing in the streets"? Next time, learn about a king who actually did that.

DANCING IN THE STREETS

It's time to bring the ark to Jerusalem. But watch out!
Touch it and you're dead! Read 2 Samuel 6:1–23 to learn
how David danced instead of dying.

Think About It
- How would you feel if you were standing beside
  Uzzah when he touched the ark?
- The ark represented the presence of God. How could it
  make David afraid and happy at the same time?
- When God does something really exciting in your life,
  what do you do to show you're happy?

Go Deeper
Read 2 Samuel 5:17–25; 1 Chronicles 16:7–36; Psalm
98:4–6; Philippians 4:4.

Prayer Starter
God is awesome, and holy, and powerful. Pray that He'll
teach you to respect Him like David did.

Facts and Fun
In 1 Kings 8:9 we read that Moses placed the two stone
tablets inside the ark. Were these the *original* Ten
Commandments or just copies?
(Answer: Copies. Moses broke the original tablets, remember?)

Coming Up Next
Have you ever made a promise that you hoped would last
forever—like, "We'll *always* be best friends"? Next time
read about such a promise God made to David.

FOREVER KINGDOM

David had his heart set on building a temple for God, but God said, "No. I want someone else to do it." Why? Read 2 Samuel 7:1–29 to find out what God told David.

Think About It

- What made David think of building a house for the Lord? What was God's response to David's attitude?
- God promised to establish a kingdom that would last forever through David. Look up God's promise to you in John 3:16. Will you have eternal life in God's "forever kingdom"? How do you know?

Go Deeper

Read 1 Chronicles 22:2–19; Matthew 1:1, 16; 2 Corinthians 1:20 to learn more about God's promises.

Prayer Starter

God had a special plan for David's kingdom, and He has a special plan for you too. Ask God to help you be like David, to love Him, and be willing to do whatever He asks.

Facts and Fun

Jesus is a descendant of King David. One of His titles in the Bible is "Son of David," and *He* is the King who has finally established a kingdom that will last forever!

Coming Up Next

Have you ever had one mistake or sin lead to another and another? Learn what happened when King David sinned and tried to cover up his sin . . . next time!

ONE SIN LEADS TO ANOTHER

David sinned with another man's wife. He knew it was wrong, but he figured he could get away with it because he was, after all, the king. Read 2 Samuel 11:1–27 to find out what happened.

Think About It

- Sins tend to build upon one another. How did David's first sin lead to the next and to the next?
- Do certain television shows or friends tempt you to do wrong (for example, to act tough, steal, or speak disrespectfully to your parents)? How can you keep them from influencing you to do wrong things?

Go Deeper

Read Genesis 4:7; 2 Samuel 9–10; 1 Kings 15:5; Matthew 6:13; 1 Corinthians 10:13.

Prayer Starter

Are you tempted to take things that don't belong to you? Ask God to help you respect other people's things and not sin.

Facts and Fun

David knew Joab was so "loyal" to him that he could bluntly order Joab to have Uriah killed, and Joab would do it. Joab was "loyal" all right. He later killed David's own son, Absalom, who was a threat to David—even though David ordered Joab to spare Absalom's life.

Coming Up Next

David was a powerful king, and he had just killed a man who stood in his way. Find out next time about a man who had the guts to tell David what he did wrong.

KING CONFESSES TO MURDER!

How would a king react to being called a murderer? The prophet Nathan was just about to find out. Read 2 Samuel 12:1–25 for the story.

Think About It

- How might David have reacted to Nathan's story if Nathan had simply accused him of murdering Uriah? How did it help to tell David about the innocent little lamb first?
- Words are cheap. How did David's actions show that he was truly sorry?
- How do you react when someone tells you that you've done something wrong?

Go Deeper

Read Psalm 51 to see how strongly David repented. Read 2 Corinthians 7:9–11; James 5:16; 1 John 1:7–9.

Prayer Starter

Ask God to help you change any wrong actions you've done into right actions. Pray the same prayer David did in Psalm 51.

Facts and Fun

David had once been a shepherd, and he had a great protective love for small, defenseless lambs. That's why he was so angry at the rich man in the parable. God knew David would have this reaction.

Coming Up Next

Despite his mistakes and sins, David was such a great king you'd think his son and grandson would be too. Wrong! Keep reading to see what happens.

1 & 2 KINGS

What's next? You're about to meet royalty, that's what! So get cleaned up! Put on your best duds, and practice your curtsy or bows—because here come the kings! At first the nation of Israel was one kingdom and Solomon was the ruler. But Solomon blew it and then it split in half. It became the northern kingdom, called Israel, and the southern kingdom, called Judah. As God promised David, one of his descendants always ruled Judah. God used prophets to turn disobedient kings back to His will. There were some good kings, but most of them were bad. When the kings sinned, the people followed them, their kingdoms became weak, and enemies were able to defeat them.

First and Second Kings records the history of that time—the evils of idol worship and what happens because of disobedience. We see how God blessed obedience and punished disobedience. In the end, the people were so disobedient that God let their enemies conquer them and take them away from their promised land.

First and Second Kings covers about 400 years. All 19 kings of the northern kingdom (Israel) worshiped idols with Omri, Ahab, and Manasseh being the worst. Not one king of Israel ever attempted to bring the people back to God.

Many of the kings of Judah were also idol worshippers and led the people into idolatry. But several kings of Judah were good kings and brought the people back to God. Asa, Jehoshaphat, Uzziah, and Jotham were good kings, but Hezekiah and Josiah were the best of the kings of Judah. They followed God and obeyed Him, and the people of the southern kingdom followed their example.

Many people think that 1 and 2 Kings were originally one book. But no one knows who wrote it. Some suggest Ezra, Ezekiel, or Baruch as possible authors.

In spite of God's enemies and the failures of His people, God accomplished His purpose of loving, caring for, and forming a nation who knew Him and His ways. God is faithful to His promises. (Abraham received land, descendants, and blessings.) God's word is true. First and Second Kings, like all of God's Word, tell part of the story of God's plan for sending His Son to take care of our sins.

Are you ready? You're about the meet the wisest king of all—Solomon.

PRAYER POWER

Do you realize how awesome it is that you can have a personal conversation with the Creator of the universe? Listen in on a king's prayer in 1 Kings 2:1–4; 3:1–15; 4:29–34.

Think About It
- Solomon only prayed for wisdom. Why do you think God answered Solomon's prayer as He did?
- Solomon prayed for others, not just for himself. Do your friends need prayer too? What can you pray for them?
- Have you ever prayed for something and God gave you more than you prayed for? What was it? What did you get?

Go Deeper
Read 1 Kings 1:5–3:28; Mark 11:24; John 15:7; 1 John 3:21–22; 5:14–15.

Prayer Starter
The reason God answers your prayers is because He loves you. Think of things that your family and friends need and ask God to help them.

Facts and Fun
Solomon either had a zoo or a very noisy palace. He had a fleet of trading ships, and every three years they brought him—among other things—chimpanzees and baboons! Can you picture him sitting on his throne trying to make important decisions with baboons and chimps howling in the background?

Coming Up Next
TIMBERRR!! Get out of the way! They're chopping down huge cedar trees! Next time, read what this is all about.

GIFTS ANYONE?

Building sites are usually noisy places with lots of hammering and sawing. The building of the temple was different. Read 1 Kings 5:1–11; 6:1–2, 7, 11–22, 37–38 for the story.

Think About It
- God blesses people with different talents—also called gifts or abilities. With what abilities was Solomon blessed and how did he use them for God?
- What abilities has God given you? Do you sing or make things? Are you good at math, or sports, or telling stories? How can you use your abilities for Him?

Go Deeper
Read Exodus 35:30–36:1; Isaiah 66:1–2; Acts 7:47–50; 1 Timothy 4:14.

Prayer Starter
Ask God what He wants you to do with your abilities. Then spend some time planning how you can do it.

Facts and Fun
The wood from cedar trees smells great! So it must have been nice walking into the temple. On top of it, Solomon covered the entire inside of the temple with gold. What a sight! A poor Israelite farmer would have been in awe at the temple.

Coming Up Next
When Solomon finished building the temple and all the people gathered to make sacrifices and pray, they *sure* weren't expecting what happened next. Read all about it . . . next time!

IS GOD ONLY IN THE TEMPLE?

It took seven years to build the temple, but when Solomon dedicated it to God, the priests couldn't even get *inside* the temple! Read 1 Kings 8:6–30; 2 Chronicles 7:1–2 to find out why.

Think About It

- During the dedication, Solomon prayed a long prayer. What were some of the things Solomon prayed for? Why do you think he prayed for the people?
- Since Jesus came we no longer need to go to a temple to pray. Because of that, where can you pray?

Go Deeper

Read 1 Corinthians 6:19–20; 1 Thessalonians 5:25; 2 Timothy 1:3; James 5:13–20.

Prayer Starter

Many Christians, when they build something or are about to start a project, dedicate it to the Lord and ask His blessing on it. Think of things and projects in your life that you can dedicate to God. Ask His blessing on them.

Facts and Fun

The temple in Jerusalem was where Jews were supposed to worship God, but a man named Onias wanted to be high priest. When the Jews wouldn't let him, he went to Egypt and built a temple there. Nice try! God didn't bless it.

Coming Up Next

It seems that King Solomon had a perfect life—everything anyone could possibly want. Next time, learn what Solomon did to spoil everything!

WORSHIP A LOVING GOD OR A COLD, HARD ROCK; IT'S YOUR CHOICE

Solomon had it all—wisdom, riches, power, God's blessings. Read 1 Kings 10:23–11:13 to find out what went wrong.

Think About It

- Solomon sinned and suffered as a result. He knew better, but he sinned anyway. Any guesses why?
- God wants to be first in your life. What things do people sometimes love so much and spend so much time with that they're like idols?
- Do you think being punished for sin is fair? Why or why not? Who knows the best way to live? You, others, or God? Why?

Go Deeper

Read Exodus 20:3; Deuteronomy 17:16–17; Nehemiah 13:23–27; Mark 8:36; Romans 6:23.

Prayer Starter

Think about what is keeping you from putting God first in your life. Ask Him to help you never make anything more important than He is in your life.

Facts and Fun

Solomon had been "beloved of God," but when he was old, he worshiped some truly evil idols. He was the smartest man on earth, so it just goes to show that *really* being smart is not having a high IQ. It's loving God.

Coming Up Next

"Raise the taxes!" "No! The people will rebel!" "Ha, ha, raise the taxes!" What's happening? Read about it . . . next time!

THE KING'S DUMB FRIENDS

When King Solomon died, his son, Rehoboam, became king, but Rehoboam had some young friends who were totally out of touch with reality. Read 1 Kings 11:41–12:24 to find out the dumb advice they gave.

Think About It
- How would the situation have been different if Rehoboam had taken the advice of the elders?
- Often the advice that parents and adults give you is different from the advice kids at school give. Why does it sometimes seem "better" to follow the advice of other kids? Is it really?
- Think of times that you followed bad advice (for example, maybe you listened to your friends say it was okay to tease kids who aren't "cool"). What happened?

Go Deeper
Read Matthew 7:12; Hebrews 6:10; James 1:27.

Prayer Starter
Do you have any friends who pressure you to do certain things that your parents have forbidden you to do? If so, pray that you can stand up to their pressure. Also ask God to show you if you should change friends.

Facts and Fun
"Knock! Knock!"
"Who's there?"
"Advise."
"Advise who?"
"Ad vise man listens to odders."

Coming Up Next
Where do you get your food and drink? Next time, learn about someone who received his dinner in a VERY strange way!

GOD DID WHAT?

"Okay, here's the deal: we have just enough flour and oil to make two little buns, and the famine is going to last a couple of years. Yup! That should last us." Read 1 Kings 16:29–33; 17:1–24 to find out what *this* is all about.

Think About It
- Who really raised the widow's son from the dead? What other kinds of miracles can God do?
- Have you ever been hungry and without food? How did God look after you?
- Does your church have a food program for people going through tough times? How can you help out?

Go Deeper
Read 1 Kings 15:1–16:28; Jeremiah 32:17; Matthew 19:26; Luke 4:25–26.

Prayer Starter
There are famines in some countries of the world right now. Pray that God will provide for the people living there.

Facts and Fun
Why did the ravens bring Elijah food to eat?
(Answer: Because he was raven-ously hungry.)

Where did the ravens get the bread and meat they brought Elijah?
(Answer: I don't know. But I bet some cooks were ravin' mad.)

Coming Up Next
Ever been to a bonfire? What was it like? Learn about God's bonfire . . . next time!

GOD IS ALL-POWERFUL

COME TO THE BIG BONFIRE

Elijah decided it was time for a big showdown against the 450 prophets of the idol Baal. King Ahab agreed. He was sure Baal's prophets would win. Read 1 Kings 18:20–46 to find out what happened.

Think About It
- Why did Elijah drench his sacrifice and the wood with water? What was the point?
- Elijah asked, "How long will you waver between two opinions?" Have you ever been confused and not known what to believe? How did you solve the problem?
- Have you ever been worried, scared, or in a bad situation? Did you remember to pray? How did it help?

Go Deeper
Read Psalm 37:3; 115:2–8; Proverbs 3:5–6; James 5:16–18.

Prayer Starter
God hears your prayers. He never sleeps, takes a vacation, or is too busy. You may not see fire from heaven, but He's there! Tell God about things that confuse you, and ask for help to know what to believe.

Facts and Fun
Another "Baal" joke Elijah might have made:
    What's the matter? Is Baal in jail and you can't bail him out?

Coming Up Next
What makes you grouchy and crabby? Learn about a big grump . . . next time!

I'M SORRY

Detective Elijah tracks down the man who murdered
Naboth! And guess who the killer is! Will he say he's sorry?
Read all about it in 1 Kings 21:4–29; 22:37!

Think About It

- What does Ahab's pouting and grumping tell you
  about him? What kind of king was he?
- Many people today act like Ahab when they don't get
  what they want. Have you ever been like Ahab? How
  and when were you like him? What happened?
- Have you ever wanted something that belonged to
  someone else? What were you tempted to do to get it?
  What happened?

Go Deeper

Read Acts 3:19; Galatians 6:7–8; 1 John 1:9.

Prayer Starter

Sometimes it's hard to say "I'm sorry" when we've done
something wrong like Ahab, yet God wants us to come to
Him when we've goofed and tell Him we are sorry. If there
is something you are sorry for, talk to Him about it.

Facts and Fun

Bible Jeopardy.
Make up questions to the following answers:

1. Jezebel
2. Ahab
3. Samaria

*(Possible answers: 1. Who married King Ahab? 2. Who in today's
Bible story was sorry for his sin? 3. Where was Ahab buried?)*

Coming Up Next

Miracles, miracles, and more miracles—the Bible is full of
them. Next time, learn about someone who performed lots
of miracles!

SIN AND REPENTANCE

MIRACLE WATCH

Ever been to a funeral? If so, think of what you saw and heard. Now read 2 Kings 2:1–18 for an awesome way to leave this life!

Think About It
- Elijah had performed a lot of miracles. But who really did them?
- Elisha wanted the same power God had given Elijah. If he had stopped following Elijah, he wouldn't have received it. Have you ever been tempted to give up when you were doing something? What happened?

Go Deeper
Read Malachi 4:5–6; Matthew 17:9–13; Luke 1:13–17.

Prayer Starter
Ask God to help you follow Him as closely as Elisha followed Elijah.

Facts and Fun
Match the correct item used in God's miracles through Elijah.

1. Ravens feed Elijah . . .	A. Fire and wind
2. The jugs were always full of . . .	B. Water and food
3. Elijah's sacrifice was hit with . . .	C. Flour and oil
4. The Jordan River parted with . . .	D. Water and fire
5. Elijah was carried off to heaven in . . .	E. A cloak

(Answers: 1. B; 2. C; 3. D; 4. E; 5. A)

Coming Up Next
"Stop! Don't eat the stew! Someone has *poisoned* it!"
"Oh, great. *Now* what'll we eat for lunch?" Find out . . . next time!

AWESOME EVENTS!

Elisha was amazing! He made bitter water drinkable, raised the dead, blinded an army, and . . . well, read about it in 2 Kings 2:19–22; 4:1–7, 32–36; 6:1–7.

Think About It

- Because of God's love, He used prophets to perform miracles in caring for His people. Which miracle do you think was the most awesome?
- God did a miracle to find a lost axhead. Why do you think He cares about the small things?
- What steps can you take to give the little things in your life to God? The big things?

Go Deeper

Read Deuteronomy 7:7–9; 2 Kings 3; 4:8–44; Matthew 6:25–34; Romans 5:8; Philippians 4:19.

Prayer Starter

Name some little "miracles" God has done for you—helping you find something, supplying money you needed. Thank Him for His love in these miracles.

Facts and Fun

Here are God's miracles through Elisha. Compare them to Elijah's.

1. Jordan River parted
2. Poisonous stew purified
3. Widow's oil multiplied
4. Dead boy raised to life
5. Jericho spring water purified
6. Prophet's food multiplied
7. Naaman healed of leprosy
8. Axhead made to float
9. Soldiers blinded

Coming Up Next

Ever have a bad pimple, rash, or boil? Next time, learn about someone who took seven dips in a muddy river to get "skin like a baby"!

GOD'S MIRACLES

HERO TAKES A MUDDY DIP

General Naaman was rich and powerful, but he was sick, and all of his wealth couldn't help him. Then he heard of someone who might be able to help. But it was an *enemy!* Read about it in 2 Kings 5:1–27.

Think About It

- There was no miracle water in the Jordan River. What really cured Naaman of his leprosy? How did Naaman's cure affect his attitude toward the true God? What does his cure tell you about God?
- The Israelite servant girl told Naaman's wife about God's power. Have you ever told anyone about God? What was their reaction?

Go Deeper

Read Luke 4:27; John 3:16; Acts 16:30–31; 1 Peter 5:6.

Prayer Starter:

Find a quiet place where no one will disturb you. Read Psalm 98 as a prayer of praise for all God has done.

Facts and Fun

Joke: Naaman and his servant are standing on the banks of the Jordan.
Naaman: "He wants me to bathe in this river seven times?"
Servant: "Is there a problem with that, sir?"
Naaman: "Yes! I only brought six clean towels."

Coming Up Next

Angels are very popular these days. There are books, movies, and TV shows about them. Learn about some real angels—a "cast of thousands" . . . next time!

GOD IS BIGGER THAN MY ENEMY

Talk about hot rods! The angels of God drive around in chariots of fire! Read 2 Kings 6:8–23 to find out about a whole army of angels ready to fight!

Think About It

- Angels are very powerful. We can't usually see them, but does that mean they're not there? Why?
- Whose work do you think angels do? What kind of work do you think it is?
- While we don't pray to angels or trust in them, do you think angels are still around helping us today? Why or why not? How might angels help you?

Go Deeper

Read 2 Kings 6:24–7:20; Psalm 103:20–21; Hebrews 1:14; Revelation 19:11–14.

Prayer Starter

Thank God for His constant love, care, and help, and for His powerful angels which protect you and help you.

Facts and Fun

Elisha was not the only one who had an army of angels to help him. Jesus could have called 12 legions of angels (Matthew 26:53) to protect Him from the Romans. How big was a legion? Each Roman legion was made up of 3,000–6,000 trained soldiers.

Coming Up Next

Next time, read about a man who was so zealous, or committed, that he was downright scary! He went so fast, he drove his chariot "like a madman."

LOOK OUT! HERE COMES JEHU!

Israel (northern kingdom) had many kings—most of them bad. Suddenly along came an extremely zealous, committed, dangerous man! And he was on God's side! Read 2 Kings 9:1–24; 10:20–31 to get the story.

Think About It
- What words would you use to describe how Jehu served God?
- God gave Jehu an assignment, and he carried it out wholeheartedly. How do you handle assignments like cleaning your room, helping in church fund-raisers, or doing homework?
- God uses all kinds of people. You don't even have to be very talented. You just have to obey. But the question is: In what ways can you serve God wholeheartedly (at school, home, or church)?

Go Deeper
Read 1 Kings 21:20–22; Isaiah 38:3; Mark 12:30; Galatians 3:3–4; Colossians 3:23.

Prayer Starter
Think about what the word "wholeheartedly" (excited, sold out) means. If you want to be excited about serving God, talk to Him about it.

Facts and Fun
Write the word "wholeheartedly" at the top of a piece of paper. Using only the letters in that word see how many words you can write (for example: *heart, really, whale, tear*).

Coming Up Next
What were some of the things you did when you were seven years old? Next time, learn about a seven-year-old who became king!

SEVEN-YEAR-OLD KING!

The oldest son of a king usually is next in line to rule. But what if all the king's sons are killed? Or *almost* all of them? Read 2 Kings 11:1–21 to find out who rules then.

Think About It

- What kind of person was Athaliah? Does the term "wicked witch" come to mind? Why did the people rejoice when she died and a new king took the throne?
- You may not be a "crown prince," but if you're a Christian, you are an adopted child of God. What kind of rights or privileges do you think that gives you?

Go Deeper

Read 2 Kings 12:1–16; Romans 8:17; 9:8; 2 Timothy 3:14–17; 1 John 3:1.

Prayer Starter

Think about being adopted by God and becoming His heir, and thank Him for choosing you.

Facts and Fun

Joash served the Lord as long as Jehoiada the high priest was alive; afterwards, he turned away from serving God. No wonder God let Jehoiada live 120 years—to keep Joash in line as long as possible.

Coming Up Next

What happens when you are warned over and over not to do something and you disobey? Are you grounded for a week? Learn what happened when a whole kingdom didn't listen to a warning . . . next time!

PUNISHMENT!

The nation of Israel started out worshiping God under good kings like David and Solomon. Then they turned away from Him. What will God do to turn them around? Or will He? Read 2 Kings 17:1–18 to get the story.

Think About It
- What finally happened to the kingdom of Israel because of their sinfulness and disobedience? Do you think God's action was fair? Why or why not?
- What happens when you disobey and don't listen to repeated warnings?
- When you sin and disobey, you suffer for it. What lessons have you learned from getting disciplined?

Go Deeper
Read Deuteronomy 4; 2 Kings 17:19–41; Jeremiah 21:14; Hosea 8:13; Acts 8:4–5, 25.

Prayer Starter
Think of times that you have sinned and ask for God's forgiveness. Then use Psalm 130 as a prayer.

Facts and Fun
Word Scramble

borntubs	mariaas	dolis
laab	haduj	dorl
lraies	narwing	shipwor

(Answers: stubborn, samaria, idols, baal, judah, lord, israel, warning, worship)

Coming Up Next
Talk about trouble! A conquering army approaches Jerusalem! What will happen? Find out . . . next time!

HURRAH FOR HEZEKIAH!

Imagine watching a video of the kings of Judah. It's depressing seeing so many bad kings. Then, just when things seem blackest . . . well, just read 2 Kings 18:1–8, 17, 28–30; 19:15–20, 32–35 to get the story.

Think About It
- What did Hezekiah do when he had some real big problems? How did he know who to turn to for help?
- What do you do when faced with tough situations? What would be the best response?
- Hezekiah could trust God because he knew Him and had followed Him for some time. What do you know about God that will help you trust Him?

Go Deeper
Read Proverbs 3:5–6; Jeremiah 17:7–8.

Prayer Starter
Think about your history with God, whether it's long or short. Tell God your favorite parts.

Facts and Fun
When the Assyrian army approached, Hezekiah decided to strengthen the city wall in the newly built areas. This was not such great news for the people who lived there. The houses that stood on the planned route of the wall were destroyed and their stones used to reinforce the wall. Imagine if that had been *your* house!

Coming Up Next
Have you ever been bored to pieces so it seemed like time stood still? Next time, learn about time going backwards!

FIFTEEN YEARS OF OVERTIME!

King Hezekiah heard some really bad news. Of course he was upset by what he heard, and he reacted by looking at the wall and weeping bitterly. But that isn't the end of the story! Read 2 Kings 20:1–11 for a surprising end.

Think About It
- Why do you think God changed His mind? Why did He make time go backwards?
- God knew exactly how Hezekiah felt before he reacted, but He loved hearing it from him. God wants to hear what's in your heart too. Has God ever answered your prayers? If so, how did that make you feel?

Go Deeper
Read Joshua 10:13a; 2 Kings 20:12–21; Psalm 139:1–6; Isaiah 38:1–22; Jeremiah 12:3; 32:27.

Prayer Starter
Think about how awesome it is that God understands everything. If you are struggling with something today, talk to Him about it.

Facts and Fun
King Hezekiah was given fifteen more years to live, and he got off to a great start by getting a couple extra hours added to the very first day! Imagine what you could do with extra hours!

Coming Up Next
Have you ever found something you didn't even know you had lost? Next time, learn about someone who found something that had been lost for years!

I FOUND IT!

Buried treasure, sunken pirate ships, and Pharaohs' tombs have been discovered hundreds of years after they were lost. Read about another amazing discovery in 2 Kings 22:1–23:8.

Think About It

- How did the people change after finding the Book (Scroll) of the Law? How did the king react? Why?
- How do you feel when you find a lost object?
- Imagine there is only one Bible in the world, and it's lost! How would you feel if you found it?

Go Deeper

Read Exodus 24:7; Joshua 8:32–35; 2 Kings 23:9–30; Psalm 119:105; Jeremiah 15:16; 2 Timothy 3:16–17.

Prayer Starter

Think of how confusing life would be if God's Word had never been found and people made up their own rules instead. Thank God that we have Bibles to tell us how to live.

Facts and Fun

Scrolls were made of papyrus reeds or "clean" animal skins. They were usually 1 foot high and up to 35 feet long. Both ends were wound on wooden rollers with handles. The writing was in narrow columns and read from right to left. Most people didn't read, so the Book of the Law was read aloud by scribes.

Coming Up Next

It's not every day that a gold-covered building burns to the ground. Read about the inferno in Jerusalem . . . next time!

JERUSALEM BURNED

Judah watched while the kingdom of Israel got clobbered. Do you think they learned a lesson from that? Well, we're about to find out! Read 2 Kings 23:36–24:4; 24:18–25:12.

Think About It
- Why did God punish the people of Judah? How could they have avoided punishment?
- How can you avoid being punished? What can you learn from other people's punishments?

Go Deeper
Read Proverbs 13:1; Isaiah 13:11; Jeremiah 32:26–35; 2 Peter 3:9.

Prayer Starter
Think about God's patience. Do you think He is fair? Has He been fair with you? Talk to Him about it.

Facts and Fun
Jesus spent a lot of time in Jerusalem—He eventually died there. Jesus predicted that Jerusalem would be destroyed again. Decode this message to see how Jesus felt about Jerusalem's destruction by filling in the vowels:
1=a; 2=e; 3=i; 4=o; 5=u.

J_r_s_l_m, h_w _ft_n _ h_v_ l_ng_d t_ g_th_r
 2 5 1 2   4   4 2 3 1 2 4 2   4 1 2

y_ _r ch_ldr_n t_g_th_r, b_t y_ _ w_r_ n_t w_ll_ng
4 5 3 2   4 2 2   5   4 5 2 2 4   3 3

(Matthew 23:37).

Coming Up Next
Sure, the Jews are back in their own land, but things are not going well at all. Next time, find out what two men did about it!

EZRA & NEHEMIAH

In the books of Ezra and Nehemiah you'll meet the traveling men. Seventy years had passed since Jerusalem was destroyed and the people were taken to Babylon. Both Ezra and Nehemiah were Jews living in Persia at the time, a time when the Jews were being allowed to return to Jerusalem. The books of Ezra and Nehemiah cover the return of God's people from captivity in Babylon to Judah. During this time, God used Persian kings and Jewish leaders to bless and discipline His people.

Ready to put your back into it? It's rebuilding time! The returning Jews had a lot of work to do. The people that already lived in Judah fought against the rebuilding they were doing. But God used Ezra, Nehemiah, and kings to bring about His plan. Cyrus, the king of Persia, gave orders for the Jewish people to be allowed to return to their native land and rebuild the temple. Other influential kings during this time were Darius and Artaxerxes. The books of Ezra and Nehemiah include letters written back and forth between the kings and the people in the land, as well as prayers.

Ezra

Ezra shows how God keeps His promises to His people. He let thousands of Jews go back to Israel to the city of Jerusalem. They fixed up the temple Solomon made, and Ezra reminded the people to follow God's laws. The Jews needed to obey God so the nations around them could see that they were God's chosen people.

Nehemiah

The temple was rebuilt first, but the walls of the city of Jerusalem still needed to be repaired. Without a wall, enemies could attack God's people! It took 52 days to fix the wall. Nehemiah helped the Jews keep working even when they wanted to quit. Nehemiah also helped them remember the Lord.

Authors

These two books are treated as one, and it is not known who wrote them. Some think Ezra might have been the writer of the book of Ezra and 1 and 2 Chronicles, and Nehemiah of the book of Nehemiah, since the authors refer to themselves in the first person. Some think several people contributed to the writing of these books of Bible history. Whoever it was, God was in charge and told them what to write.

HOMECOMING

How would you feel if you and thousands of your relatives got together for a huge family reunion—and then *walked* a thousand miles to a strange land and stayed there? Read 2 Chronicles 36:22–23; Ezra 1:1–11 to meet some people who did just that.

Think About It
- God gave King Cyrus a job to do and he did it. How do you think the Jewish people felt about King Cyrus?
- What are some responsibilities you've been given at home or in school? Why were you given these responsibilities? Think about it.
- Not all jobs and responsibilities are interesting and fun. How faithful are you with boring jobs that need to be done?

Go Deeper
Read Ecclesiastes 9:10; Isaiah 45:11–13; Colossians 3:22–23.

Prayer Starter
What are some things you are responsible for? Feeding the pet? Delivering newspapers? Washing dishes? Ask God to help you do all your jobs faithfully.

Facts and Fun
When the teacher said she needed someone responsible, Tim shot his hand into the air.

The teacher asked, "Tim, are you responsible?"

"I must be," he said. "Whenever something goes wrong at home, my mom says I'm responsible."

Coming Up Next
How do you feel when you really "blow it" and then you are given a second chance? Next time, learn how the Jews felt about their second chance!

GOODNESS, MERCY, AND SHIRLEY?

The Jewish people were back in the Promised Land! They hadn't been there long when their neighbors heard a confusing roar. What was that all about? Read Ezra 2:64–69; 3:1–13.

Think About It
- Having the temple again was a sign of God's presence and a reminder that He was their loving God. How do you think the Jews felt when the temple was rebuilt?
- Imagine if you'd been far away from someone who loved you, and then they came back. How would you feel?
- God was giving His people a second chance. If you were one of them, what would you have done?

Go Deeper
Read 1 Chronicles 21:13; Psalm 126:5; Haggai 2:8.

Prayer Starter
When have you received a second chance (to make the team, use something you once broke)? Well, God gives us second chances too. Thank God for that.

Facts and Fun
The Sunday school teacher read the Twenty-third Psalm, "Surely goodness and mercy will follow me all the days of my life."

Trevor said, "I understand about having goodness and mercy, because God is good. But I'm not sure I'd like Shirley following me around all the time."

Coming Up Next
Ever had someone who hated you and did everything they could to make your life miserable? Next time, learn about some people like that.

HAMMER, HAMMER, SAW, SAW

King Artaxerxes, supreme ruler of the Persian Empire, gave a direct order to the Jews: Stop building the temple! Immediately! Read Ezra 4:1–8, 17–24; 5:1–5; 6:3, 7–9 to find out what happened when two men challenged that order.

Think About It
- What gave the people the courage to keep building the temple even when their neighbors were discouraging them? What was the result?
- What things, or discouraging words, can stop you from finishing a project? What would help you keep going?
- When faced with a mountain, you can quit. Or you can climb over it, go around it, or tunnel through it. Which do you do when faced with a mountain or discouraging words from others?

Go Deeper
Read Joshua 1:9; Ezra 6:13–7:10; Psalm 27:14.

Prayer Starter
Are you discouraged because people tell you that you're not able to do something? Pray that God will give you the courage to keep going.

Facts and Fun
Parts of the book of Ezra are written in Aramaic—the official language of that day—not Hebrew. Why? Because Ezra was so intent on quoting official documents *accurately* that he quoted them word for word in *Aramaic!*

Coming Up Next
Are you part of a team? Learn about a winning team . . . next time!

WINNING TEAM

Why is teamwork important on a sports team? What happens when every player wants to do "his own thing"? Read Nehemiah 1:1–4; 2:11–20; 4:1–13; 9:2–3, 32–38 to find out about winning teamwork.

Think About It

- Building the wall was a team project. What made Nehemiah and the other people have a winning team?
- Team players have the same goals and values. What kind of people or friends have the same values and goals as you?
- If you play on a team, what difference does having the same goals make? How does it affect your willingness to help each other?

Go Deeper

Read Nehemiah 5:1–6:16; Psalm 127:1; Ecclesiastes 4:9–12.

Prayer Starter

Thank God for the people who are your teammates, people who share your values and goals. Ask Him for more friends to work together with you.

Facts and Fun

Nehemiah was a cupbearer. A cupbearer tasted the king's wine first to make sure it wasn't poisoned. What a job! Fortunately, King Artaxerxes' enemies never got close enough to poison his wine, so Nehemiah lived to supervise the rebuilding of Jerusalem's wall.

Coming Up Next

Have you ever been in a spelling bee, a gunnysack race, or a beauty contest? Learn about a Bible-time beauty contest . . . next time!

ESTHER

Do you enjoy suspense, mystery, and intrigue? Those are big words, but you probably know what they are—they're what make you want to keep reading a good book or watching an exciting movie.

The book of Esther is an action-packed thriller! It has plots and counterplots, villains and heroes, humor and justice. It's about a beautiful Jewish girl named Esther, who became a courageous queen. She was used by God to save the entire Jewish nation from being murdered.

Banquets and Plots

The book begins with a banquet and ends with the Festival of Purim, which is still observed by the Jewish people today. Purim is a happy celebration of remembering and thanking God for saving and caring for His people. In the middle of the book, Mordecai foils a plot against the king, and Haman hatches one to destroy the Jews.

Who Wrote It

No one knows who wrote the book. Some think Esther's cousin, Mordecai, is the author. God is never mentioned in the book of Esther, yet He is behind everything that happens in it. Esther is never mentioned in the New Testament either. The book of Esther is one of two Old Testament books named for a woman. The other one is Ruth.

If the Jewish nation had not been saved, we would have never had a Savior. Without a Savior the world would have been lost. God's plan was for Esther to pave the way for the world's Savior. God used Esther just like He used Joseph and Abraham and others to bring about His plan.

WANTED: GORGEOUS GIRL TO BE QUEEN

"Listen, Esther. The king is looking for a new queen. He might pick you, so do not—I repeat, do *not*—under any circumstances, tell him who you really are!" What's this all about? Read Esther 1:10–12; 2:1–11, 15–20 to find out.

Think About It

- Sure, Esther was beautiful. But so were all the other women the king had to choose from. Who really influenced the king in his choice?
- Whose advice did Esther rely on when she was taken to the king? Why?
- Sometimes you have to do a huge job and need the wise advice of older people to help you. When has this happened in your life?

Go Deeper

Read Esther 2; Psalm 139:15–16; 145:13; Proverbs 1:7.

Prayer Starter

Think about how God put Esther in the right place. Talk to God about times He's put you in the right place, like being there when someone needed help.

Facts and Fun

Kings used to have many wives. They lived together in a wing of the palace where no outside men could go. The wives usually lived in great luxury.

Coming Up Next

Just being beautiful isn't enough. Learn what Esther needed besides her beauty . . . next time!

BEAUTY, BRAINS, AND BRAVERY

Crazy law, but here's what it said: No one can approach the king without an appointment—not even the queen. Try it and you're dead. But Esther took her chances. Read Esther 3:1–9; 4:8–14; 5:1–4; 7:1–6, 10; 8:11.

Think About It
- How did Esther prepare herself? How do you prepare for an important or difficult task?
- Esther was the perfect person to do that job. Have you ever been the perfect person to do a job? What was it?
- Have you ever *had* to do something dangerous? Did you pray for help? What happened?

Go Deeper
Read Esther 6; 8–9; Psalm 37:1–6; Hebrews 11:1, 6.

Prayer Starter
Christians in some countries are persecuted for their faith. Pray for persecuted Christians and ask God to protect them.

Facts and Fun
Hamantashen is a three-cornered cookie eaten during Purim, the Jewish festival celebrating Esther's saving of the Jews. It is thought that Haman wore a three-cornered hat, something like these cookies.

1 cup of butter—1 cup sugar—4 eggs—1 orange (grated rind and juice)—1/4 cup water—1 teaspoon vanilla—4 cups flour—4 teaspoons baking soda—1 teaspoon salt—Filling: Your favorite prepared fruit filling.

Cream the butter and sugar. Beat together eggs, orange rind, juice, water, and vanilla. Add to butter and sugar and mix together. Sift dry ingredients together. Add dry ingredients to mixture and stir. Refrigerate overnight. Roll out a little at a time on a well-floured board. Cut in rounds, fill, and pinch three corners together. Bake at 375 degrees for 25 minutes.

Coming Up Next
We're about to do a time warp from the Old Testament to the New. So, get your space goggles and hunker down to find out what happens when a baby is born . . . next time!

THE GOSPELS: LUKE & JOHN

A tiny baby born in a stall—what does that have to do with 2,000 years of world and Bible history? Everything! That baby was the end goal of all the Old Testament preparations. Everything was now ready for what God promised Adam and Eve, Abraham, and David.

In Luke and John you will meet glorious angels, loyal friends, and huge crowds. You will also mingle with the sick, disabled, demon-possessed, and a few dead people. A grown man learns how to be born again, a short man climbs a tree, and a boy shares his lunch.

You will see that Jesus is a good friend. He is kind and loving to everyone, healing the sick, and helping those in need. Listen as Jesus teaches God's Word with wonderful stories about seeds, lost sons, and rich fools. Hear Him say that He is the Vine, the Living Water, the Good Shepherd, and the Bread of Life—names that tell us more about Jesus and who He is.

Who Wrote These Books

Both these books, Luke and John, are named for their authors. Luke was a companion of Paul the apostle, not one of Jesus' twelve disciples. Luke was probably a Gentile medical doctor. John was one of Jesus' disciples. John always called himself the disciple whom Jesus loved. The book of Luke is thought to have been written A.D. 59–63 and the book of John was probably written A.D. 85 or later.

What to Look for in Luke and John

Luke explains and gives more details to some of the stories found in Matthew and Mark. There are more stories about Jesus' birth and early life in Luke, and it's the only book with the parable of the Good Samaritan. Since Luke was not Jewish, he includes stories that show Jesus' interest in the non-Jewish world and the poor. Luke gives the greatest variety of teaching, parables, and events from the life of Jesus.

John records seven miracles, climaxing in Jesus' resurrection, which he sees as proof that Jesus is the Son of God. John also includes several sermons of Christ not found in the other Gospels, which explain the purpose of Jesus' life. The shortest verse in the Bible is found in John 11:35.

ONE-OF-A-KIND KID!

Is the Christmas story still exciting and wonderful for you? The Old Testament said lots of things about the Savior's birth and life, and every prophecy came true! Read Luke 1:5–20, 26–38 to find out more about this.

Think About It
- Mary knew Jesus was God's Son because the angel told her about Jesus' birth and who He was before He was born. How do you think Mary felt being the mother of God's child?
- Zechariah had trouble believing—even when an *angel* appeared and told him! Do you sometimes have trouble believing God will do good things for you? Why?

Go Deeper
Read Luke 1:39–80; 3:22; John 1:1–2.

Prayer Starter
Thank God for caring enough to plan things out so carefully for thousands of years. Thank Him for His plans for you too.

Facts and Fun
Hundreds of thousands of angels carry out God's commands. But Gabriel is one of only two angels mentioned by name in the Bible. Michael (Daniel 10:13; 12:1) is the other. Gabriel's name means "God is my hero/warrior."

Coming Up Next
Have you ever waited for something really big and time just seemed to drag along? Next time, learn about people who had been waiting for thousands of years!

FINALLY! THE MAIN CHARACTER

How did a Roman king, an innkeeper, heavenly angels, and poor shepherds all become part of an astonishing birth? And who is the *main* character? Read Luke 2:1–22 to find out.

Think About It
- If you were planning who the angels appeared to, would you have sent them first to ordinary people like shepherds? Why or why not?
- The Bible is one big story tying together what was promised long ago and what is now happening. Whose story is it? What can you do to spread the big story of God's love and forgiveness?

Go Deeper
Read Isaiah 9:6–7; Micah 5:2; Matthew 2:1–23; Luke 2:23–40.

Prayer Starter
Think of your favorite Christmas carols and use one as your prayer. Listen to it, sing it, or read it, thinking about what the words mean.

Facts and Fun
All through the Old Testament, God promised to send a Savior, the Messiah. The Bible said that He would be born from the line of King David, that His mother would be a virgin, and even that He would be born in Bethlehem. Jesus fulfilled *all* of these promises!

Coming Up Next
Did you ever get separated from your family? Next time, learn about a boy who was alone in a strange place for three days!

I'M RIGHT AT HOME HERE

Have you ever wondered what Jesus did when He was a kid? Did He play games, do chores, and go to school? Probably. But the Bible actually only tells about one thing Jesus did when He was a boy. Read Luke 2:41–52 to find out what that was.

Think About It
- Jesus stayed in the temple three days. How does His answer to Mary tell you how He felt about being there? How do you feel about reading your Bible and learning about God? Who do you want to be with when you go to church?
- Even Jesus was obedient to His parents! How do you think He wants you to relate to your parents?

Go Deeper
Read Exodus 13:3, 10, 14–16; Deuteronomy 6:1–7; Psalm 119:99–100; Proverbs 1:8.

Prayer Starter
Many of the Psalms were worship songs used in the temple. Read Psalm 100 or 150 (or both of them) as praise prayers to the Lord.

Facts and Fun
Two messages on a church signboard:
Sunday morning sermon: "Jesus Walking on Water"
Sunday evening sermon: "Looking for Jesus"

Coming Up Next
Think of the sneakiest, biggest liar you have ever been around. Learn of a mean low-down character that is a hundred times worse than whoever you thought of . . . next time!

I DARE YOU TO JUMP!

Ever wonder about Satan—who he is and why he stirs up trouble? Discover the biggest challenge Satan ever faced in Luke 3:21–22; 4:1–13.

Think About It

- When Satan tempted Jesus, how did Jesus resist?
- Satan often uses people or things as temptations. Can you think of some people who may tempt you to do something wrong? What things or activities tempt you?
- God always loves and cares for you. How can knowing this help you when you are tempted?

Go Deeper

Read Matthew 3:1–4:11; Luke 3:1–23; 1 Corinthians 10:13; 1 Peter 5:8–9.

Prayer Starter

Talk to God about things that tempt you to sin, such as videos, TV shows, or kids who do wrong. Ask God for His help in resisting them.

Facts and Fun

Once Satan was an angel but he rebelled against God and was thrown out of heaven. Now Satan hates God and is trying to tempt everyone away from Him. Jesus' death on the cross defeated Satan, and Jesus gives us the power to resist his temptations.

Coming Up Next

Did you ever wish you could be an entirely different person and have lots of new friends? Learn about a man who did just that . . . next time!

DID YOU HEAR AND SEE THAT?

Do you daydream about what you will do when you grow up? Do your parents have plans for you? God had plans for His Son, Jesus. Read them in Luke 4:14–15, 40–44; 5:27–32; 6:12–16; 8:1–3.

Think About It
- God's plan for Jesus was to show people what God is like. How did Jesus' teaching and healing do that?
- Think of some people you know who no one likes. How can you be like Jesus and show them God's love?
- Imagine you are Matthew the tax collector. What would it have been like to go through such a huge change?

Go Deeper
Read 1 Samuel 1:24–28; Psalm 139:1–3; Luke 4:14–5:11.

Prayer Starter
Think about your plans and dreams for the future and talk to God about them. Then ask for God's help in finding and following His plan for your life.

Facts and Fun
In Jesus' day, tax collectors were unpopular. In the movie *Jesus of Nazareth*, when the tax collector Matthew was explaining, "I am also called Levi," Simon Peter added, "And many other names as well!"

Coming Up Next
Have you ever heard the expression "Lose the roof over your head"? Learn about some people who actually had that experience . . . next time!

LOOK OUT BELOW!

Do you know someone who has a very serious disease? If they needed to see a doctor, would you rip off the hospital roof to get them in? Read in Luke 5:12–26; 17:11–19 how one man's friends did just that!

Think About It
- The friends of the paralyzed man wanted to help him, and obviously they weren't very shy. How did they show their faith in Jesus?
- Sometimes you can help people in need just by being kind. What are other ways you can help them?
- What do you do when Jesus helps you get well when you've been sick? Are you like the nine lepers or the one?

Go Deeper
Read Mark 1:40–2:12; Acts 9:36; James 1:27.

Prayer Starter
Think about people in your church, school, or neighborhood who are in need. Pray for them and ask God to show you how you can help—then do it.

Facts and Fun
In Bible times leprosy was a feared disease because it was highly contagious and incurable. People treated lepers with disgust and as outcasts. They had to live by themselves and call out "Unclean" when someone came near them.

Coming Up Next
Most Jews expected the Messiah to be a fighting warrior king who would slaughter their enemies. Next time, find out what He was *really* like!

LISTEN UP!

Think about the least likeable people you know—a bully, an obnoxious kid, or someone unattractive. Do you have to love them? Read Luke 6:20–36, 43–49 to find out.

Think About It
- Jesus said, "Do to others as you would have them do to you." Is that hard or easy for you? Why? How would you like others to treat you?
- How do you feel when you're used to treating people a certain way, and then read in the Bible that you're supposed to do the *opposite?*

Go Deeper
Read Matthew 5:3–12; Luke 6:1–16, 37–42; 7:1–35; 1 Corinthians 5:13–21; 2 Timothy 3:16–17.

Prayer Starter
Luke 6:31 is called the Golden Rule. Think of someone you need to treat better and ask for God's help and for opportunities to be kind to that person.

Facts and Fun
Some people think they're funny by saying that the Golden Rule is, "He who has the gold, makes the rules." But God *made* all the gold on earth, and His city in heaven is made out of solid gold (Revelation 21:18). And that's why *God* gets to make the rules!

Coming Up Next
What if your dad or grandpa could be reborn? Wouldn't that be amazing? Next time, learn about a grown man who was born again!

GROWN MAN IS BORN AGAIN!

If you really wanted to talk to someone but were afraid
the others would make fun of you, how would you do it?
Secretly, right? Read about a secret night meeting in
John 3:1–21.

Think About It

- People in Jesus' day thought they had to obey the
  entire Law of Moses to please God. Some people today
  think doing good or having Christian parents saves
  them from sin and hell. Wrong! What is the only way
  to be saved?
- If you believe that Jesus is the only way to God, how
  important does this make His commands about how
  we should live?

Go Deeper

Read John 1:12–13; 14:6; Romans 8:9–11; 2 Corinthians
5:13–21.

Prayer Starter

Thank God that *everyone* is welcome to be "born again."
Pray for friends who aren't Christians to be "born again."

Facts and Fun

Nicodemus was an "undercover" believer, afraid of people
knowing he was Jesus' follower. But as he came to know
Jesus, he became bolder. In fact, after soldiers tried to arrest
Jesus, Nicodemus spoke up for Him. And after Jesus' death,
Nicodemus helped bury Him.

Coming Up Next

Are there certain kinds of people that your neighbors don't
like? Would you go out of your way to be friends with
those people? Find out what one man did . . . next time!

STRANGER AT THE TOWN WELL

Talk about radical! Jesus not only visited people the Jews *hated*, He made friends with the most unpopular person in town! Read John 4:5–26, 39–42.

Think About It
- Jesus shared the Good News with unpopular people. Who might He want *you* to talk with about Him?
- Think of what Jesus means to you and what He has done for you. How can you put that into a message for others?

Go Deeper
Read Luke 9:51–56; 10:30–37; 17:11–19; John 1:40–51; Acts 1:7–8; 1 Peter 3:15.

Prayer Starter
Pour a glass of water. Think how important it is for your life. Then think of the "living water" Jesus gives you and thank Him for it. Ask God to help you share your faith with others.

Facts and Fun
Jews and Samaritans were related, but they sure didn't get along. Jews traveling between Judea and Galilee tried to never go through Samaria. They would cross the Jordan, head north, then cross back above Samaria—even if it meant an extra day's journey.

Coming Up Next
Pulling rabbits out of hats, making things disappear— those are "magic" tricks. But when you need the real thing, who do you go to? Find out what an army captain did . . . next time!

UTTERLY AWESOME HAPPENINGS!

To whom do you go for help when you're in trouble? How do they help you? Read about some of the people who came to Jesus for help in Luke 7:1–17; 8:22–25.

Think About It
- The centurion was sure that Jesus had all the love and power of God available to Him. If you were as sure of that as the centurion was, what would you do the next time you needed help?
- Imagine you were one of Jesus' disciples in the boat. What would you have been thinking?

Go Deeper
Read Luke 8:26–56; 9:37–43; John 10:25; 17:3.

Prayer Starter
Think of the things in your life you're most thankful for. Then thank God for these things and for all He does for you. Thank Him for being there when you need Him.

Facts and Fun
Mother: "There were two popsicles in the freezer this morning. Can you explain why there's *one* there now?"
Son: "I guess I just didn't see it."

Coming Up Next
Ever been so hungry that it sounded as though you had a roaring lion in your stomach? Learn about a whole hillside full of rumbling stomachs . . . next time!

WHAT'S FOR LUNCH?

Adults can be pretty spacey sometimes. Five thousand men spent the day in the desert, but it seems only one young boy remembered to bring a lunch. Read John 6:1–21 to learn about a HUGE hunger problem.

Think About It
- Have you ever wondered what it would be like to be the boy who gave Jesus his lunch? What might *he* have thought when he saw Jesus' miracle?
- Walking on water! Wow! Now that's some miracle! Just how did Jesus get such miraculous power?

Go Deeper
Read Matthew 6:25–34; 7:7–12; 15:29–39; Luke 9:10–17.

Prayer Starter
Tell God about your number one need and ask Him to help you trust Him to take care of it and everything else. Thank God for meeting all your needs.

Facts and Fun
Picnic for 5,000: For each person to get just one burger, one small serving of chips, and one glass of lemonade, you would need 839 bags of chips, 313 gallons of lemonade, 625 packages of buns, and 1,250 pounds of hamburger, not to mention a wheelbarrow full of butter, ketchup, and relish! You would need a parade of grocery carts for that shopping trip!

Coming Up Next
By the time *this* woman was finished crying, Jesus' feet were squeaky clean! Next time, read about a lady armed with a perfume bottle.

TEARS, PERFUME, AND LONG HAIR

When you hear about people doing horrible things, do you wonder if God can forgive them? Do you worry that you've done something so bad that God won't forgive you? Read Luke 7:36–50 and meet a woman who felt that way.

Think About It
- Suppose you had been at the table eating. Would you have been embarrassed by the woman? Why do you think she didn't bother Jesus?
- How would Jesus want you to treat people that you think are too sinful? How easy or hard is it for you to be kind to them?

Go Deeper
Read Isaiah 1:18; Luke 1:76–77; 17:1–4; John 12:1–8.

Prayer Starter
Jesus told us not to judge others, yet we're tempted to do just that. Who do you judge? Ask God to give you more love and less criticism for that person.

Facts and Fun
Connor came home from Sunday school looking very upset.
"What's wrong?" asked his mom.
"I thought Jesus was nice," he said.
"Oh, He is," Mom answered.
"Well, I don't know," said Connor. "Teacher says Jesus takes away all my sins and He NEVER gives them back!"

Coming Up Next
Would you want to bunk down with the pigs and fight with them for scraps? Learn a story about someone who did that . . . next time!

SEEDS AND SWINE

Did you ever do something stupid or selfish and then try to convince yourself that it was okay? But then did you feel bad and weren't sure what to do next? You're not alone! Read Luke 8:4–15; 15:11–24.

Think About It
- Jesus said that life's concerns and pleasures are like thorns that try to stop you from living for God. What "thorns" are trying to choke you?
- The prodigal son didn't care about his father or the farm. All he cared about was having a good time. Have you been like that? How?
- Imagine the son's surprise when he apologized and his dad threw a party for him. How is God like that dad?

Go Deeper
Read Psalm 37:4–5; Proverbs 16:3.

Prayer Starter
Most of us have gone our own selfish way and had to apologize. Think of times this has happened and ask God to keep you faithful and strong.

Facts and Fun
Daffy Definitions
Who was Joan of Arc?
(Answer: Noah's wife)
Who wrote Psalms?
(Answer: Psalmbody)
What are the epistles?
(Answer: Wives of the apostles)

Coming Up Next
Sometimes really strong men bend iron bars and tear telephone books in half. Learn about a man who makes them look like weaklings . . . next time!

STRONGER THAN DEMONS

Do you wonder how powerful Satan is? Does he have helpers to cause problems for believers? Read about some of Satan's henchmen in Luke 8:22–39.

Think About It

- How would you describe the demon-possessed man before Jesus came to him? How did he change after meeting Jesus?
- How do you feel when you think of Jesus' power? How does knowing Jesus is stronger than demons help you?

Go Deeper

Read Matthew 15:21–28; Mark 16:9; Luke 4:40–41; 6:17–19.

Prayer Starter

Thank God for being stronger than Satan and for giving you peace in even the worst situations. Tell Him about things that upset you or make you afraid. Remember that God cares for you and will hear your prayer.

Facts and Fun

Abyss: The New Testament uses this word once for the place of the dead (Romans 10:7 NKJV). More often it describes a "bottomless pit" where Satan and evil spirits will be confined (Revelation 20:3 NKJV).

Coming Up Next

Did you ever have a neighbor come and wake up your whole family at midnight because he wanted to borrow a loaf of bread? No? Well read all about a neighbor who did . . . next time!

HI, GOD! IT'S ME!

Judge: "Okay, what's the next case?" Guard: "Uh . . . It's uh . . ." Judge: "No! Not *her* again! The *widow?*" Guard: "I'm afraid so, your honor." What's this about? Read Luke 11:1–13; 18:1–8 to find out.

Think About It

- Have you ever been like the loaf-less friend or persistent widow when you pray? What do you really need from God?
- Sometimes God doesn't answer our prayers the way we want. Why do you think He answers differently from the way we expect?

Go Deeper

Read Matthew 7:11; John 17:1–26; Ephesians 6:18.

Prayer Starter

One way to remember to share all things with God is to pray an ACTS prayer.

Adoration—Tell God how wonderful He is.
Confession—Admit your sins to God.
Thanksgiving—Thank God for all He's done.
Supplication—Ask for something.

Facts and Fun

Mom was teaching three-year-old Matthew to say the Lord's Prayer. Mom said a phrase and Matthew repeated it.
Mom: "Give us this day our daily bread."
Matthew: "And please don't forget the peanut butter and jelly!"

Coming Up Next

Do you know people who have nicknames that tell something unusual about them? Next time, meet someone who described himself like something straight out of a bakery.

MODERN-DAY MANNA

Some people liked the loaves and fish Jesus had fed them, so they followed Him wanting more. Read John 6:25–40, 63 to find out what Jesus offered them to eat next!

Think About It

- Jesus said He was "the bread from heaven." Think about how important and basic bread is to life. Why do you think Jesus called Himself bread?
- Jesus said His words are "spirit and life." They make us alive. They charge our batteries. Have you ever read something from the Bible that excited or strengthened you? What?

Go Deeper

Read Exodus 16:11–15; Deuteronomy 8:16; Psalm 78:23–25; 119:9–16; Matthew 11:27.

Prayer Starter

How many days would a loaf of bread satisfy you if you ate one sandwich a day? Thank Jesus, the "Bread of Life," for all the needs He satisfies.

Facts and Fun

Jesus calls Himself "I am" seven times: "I am" the Bread of Life; the Light of the World; the Gate; the Good Shepherd; the Resurrection and the Life; the Way, the Truth, and the Life; and the True Vine. Each of these names tells us something about Him.

Coming Up Next

Have you ever been in a dark place and tried to read? Or tried to walk in the dark and bumped into a wall? Learn about two kinds of blindness . . . next time!

WOW! I CAN SEE!

Light is what makes seeing possible (just try pinning the tail on the donkey while wearing a thick blindfold). But there's more than one kind of light and sight. Read John 9:1–21, 30–31, 34–41 and you'll see.

Think About It
- Imagine you are the blind man. You've never seen before, but now you can. What would you think?
- The former blind man didn't care if everyone rejected him. He believed in Jesus and stood up for Him. In what situations would you like to have that kind of enthusiasm?

Go Deeper
Read Mark 8:22–26; Luke 18:35–43; John 20:29; 1 Peter 1:8.

Prayer Starter
Thank Jesus for being the Light of the World and showing you the truth about Himself and what He has done. Ask for help to have even more faith in Him.

Facts and Fun
When is spitting like plowing a field? On the Sabbath! The Pharisees had many rules to make sure people didn't work on the Sabbath. One was "no spitting allowed." It might move some dirt, and that would be plowing!

Coming Up Next
Imagine you're lost in a crowd in a foreign city when suddenly you hear your dad calling your name! What a relief! Read about things like that . . . next time.

FOLLOW YOUR EARS

Picture a poster in the sheep pen telling sheep why they should go with the shepherd. What would it say? Well, sheep can't read, but they do follow the shepherd's voice! Read John 10:1–18, 27–29 to discover the best Shepherd ever.

Think About It

- You are a sheep and Jesus is your Shepherd, so if Satan attacks like a lion, Jesus will protect you. How does that make you feel?
- What happens to sheep who wander off into Wolf Land? What problems can you avoid by staying close to Jesus?

Go Deeper

Read Psalm 23; 119:105–112; Ezekiel 34:1–24; Luke 15:1–7.

Prayer Starter

Read Psalm 23 and think about how great it is to be part of the Good Shepherd's flock! Thank Jesus for being your Shepherd.

Facts and Fun

A sheepfold was made of four stone walls with one entrance. Thorns on the top discouraged wolves and other animals from crawling in to attack the sheep. The shepherd slept in front of the opening to protect the flock and keep them from wandering off.

Coming Up Next

Taking care of a vineyard is hard work, but it sure is worth it when you see those big, juicy grapes! Learn where the best possible grapes are . . . next time!

HANG ON TIGHT!

There were many vineyards in Palestine, so Jesus often talked about them to teach important stories about God and living as God wants us to. Read John 15:1–17 to learn how following Jesus is like being a big bunch of grapes!

Think About It

- Imagine how a clump of grapes that "walked off" from the vine would be shriveled raisins before it got ten miles. How would you be effected if you were suddenly ten miles from Jesus?
- If you stay hooked up to the true vine (Jesus' love) you'll have the power to love others, not give in to temptation, etc. What areas of your life do you need more power and love in?

Go Deeper

Read Psalm 80:8–11; Isaiah 5:1–7; 1 Corinthians 13:4–8; Galatians 5:22–23.

Prayer Starter

Print each Fruit of the Spirit found in Galatians 5:22–23 on paper. Think about each one and thank God for the fruit that you have in your life. Then ask for His help in developing the fruit you're missing or weak in.

Facts and Fun

"Knock! Knock!"
"Who's there?"
"Vine."
"Vine who?"
"Vine you come out and climb over the wall with me?"

Coming Up Next

Do you know someone who is wonderfully different from most others? Learn about someone VERY special . . . next time!

SOMETHING SPECIAL ABOUT JESUS!

Imagine you were on the mountain with Jesus and two other disciples. You knew Jesus was special, but then an amazing, awesome thing happened that just about stunned you! Read Luke 9:18–36 to find out what it was.

Think About It
- Some people thought Jesus was just a prophet teaching them how to live. Why is it very important that He's not just a prophet, but the Savior?
- Who do you believe Jesus is? Do you believe He has saved you from your sins? Why?

Go Deeper
Read Matthew 3:17; 14:33; Mark 9:2–8; Luke14:25–35.

Prayer Starter
Read Luke 3:21–22. Think of ways you can be Jesus' disciple, follow His teachings, and tell others about Him. Ask God to help you do this.

Facts and Fun
A young girl went to her pastor and confessed, "I'm so proud that it's a sin."

"Why do you think that?" the minister asked.

"Because every time I look in the mirror I think how beautiful I am."

"Oh, I wouldn't worry," the minister assured her. "That isn't a sin. It's only a mistake."

Coming Up Next
How do people usually feel at a funeral? Learn about some people that had a huge surprise at a grave . . . next time!

SURPRISING ANSWER

Jesus healed many people, so when His friend Lazarus was sick, Lazarus' sisters begged Jesus to heal him. Jesus didn't come. Lazarus died. End of story? Read John 11:17–44.

Think About It

- Lazarus was stone-cold dead. Imagine you were there. What would people think when he walked out of the tomb?
- Lazarus was sick, but Jesus only arrived after he'd been dead three days. Have you ever had to wait a long time for an answer to prayer? How did you feel and what did you do?

Go Deeper

Read Mark 5:22–24, 38–42; Luke 10:38–42; John 11:1–16, 45–57; 12:1–11, 37–50; Philippians 4:6.

Prayer Starter

God *can* heal the sick. But He doesn't always do what we ask. Ask God to help you trust Him even when He doesn't answer your prayers the way you would like.

Facts and Fun

Bible-time burials: The body was washed and tightly wrapped in grave clothes and spices, and a linen cloth was placed over the face. Tombs were caves or rooms with a flat, heavy stone rolled against the opening.

Coming Up Next

What would you do if you were walking along the road and found an injured person? Learn about someone who faced that situation . . . next time!

TRAVELER HELPS HIS ENEMY

Beaten, bleeding, and lying in the ditch—what a pitiful sight! He was probably close to dying. Who would help him? Read Luke 10:25–37 for the story.

Think About It

- What reasons might the Jewish priest and Levite have given for not stopping and helping him? Why do you think the Samaritan stopped and gave the man everything he needed? What did the Samaritan get out of it?
- What are some things that stop you from helping others?
- What difference will faith *and* actions make to someone you help? To you?

Go Deeper

Read Matthew 22:34–40; 25:31–46; James 2:14–17; 1 John 3:17–19; 4:20–21.

Prayer Starter

Thank God for people who are kind and helpful and show their faith by their deeds. Talk to God about people who you could be friends with and ask Him to help you do that.

Facts and Fun

Do an acrostic puzzle using the word FAITH. Put the letters down the side of a paper and think of faith-proving deeds that start with each letter (for example: F=food for hungry, friendliness, etc.).

Coming Up Next

Do you know someone who thinks he or she is better than everyone else? Learn about a whole group of people who had that attitude . . . next time!

LOOK HOW GOOD I AM!

Have you ever met people who acted so "righteous" and "holy" that they were . . . well . . . weird to be around? Jesus talked a lot about that kind of people. Read Luke 11:37–54; 18:9–14 and see!

Think About It
- What was the attitude of the tax collector? Who would you rather be like, the Pharisee or the tax collector who repented? Why?
- People who are proud of how righteous they are are a pain! But we're *all* tempted at times to think we're great. C'mon, 'fess up! When have *you* acted this way?

Go Deeper
Read Hosea 14:9; Matthew 4:19; Mark 7:1–23; Luke 20:9–19.

Prayer Starter
Pray like the tax collector, asking for mercy and thanking God for His forgiveness. Ask for help in choosing God's way.

Facts and Fun
Imagine a Pharisee who was *so* "righteous" that he carefully tithed all his tiny, tiny mustard seeds. It took him three months, but he finally had 360,000,000 seeds in a pile for himself, and 40,000,000 seeds for God. And then he sneezed.

Coming Up Next
What do you do when you have so many things that you don't have enough room to store them all? Read the answer . . . next time.

LOTS OF BARNS BUT NO BRAINS

Do you ever wonder what should be most important in your life? Read Luke 12:13–34 to find out what Jesus says about that.

Think About It

- Imagine that you are the rich fool. What are some things that could become too important to you? What are some things you might spend too much of your time and energy on?
- The man who asked the question and the man in the story were thinking only of earthly treasures, but Jesus said to focus on treasures in heaven, such as eternal life. How can you get this?

Go Deeper

Read Psalm 1; Luke 12:1–11; Ephesians 5:1–11.

Prayer Starter

Think of some situations you face where you need to make a choice. Ask for God's help in choosing the right thing and focusing on treasures in heaven.

Facts and Fun

"Knock! Knock!"
"Who's there?"
"Luke."
"Luke who?"
"Luke at me jump rope."

"Knock! Knock!"
"Who's there?"
"John."
"John who?"
"Want to John me in a game of basketball?"

Coming Up Next

Have you ever tried to get a thread through the eye of a needle? Want to watch people try something even harder? Then tune in . . . next time!

A NEEDLE'S EYE

It's not a sin to be rich, but it *is* a sin to live selfishly and not care for the poor. Read Luke 16:19–31; 18:18–30 to discover what Jesus said about this.

Think About It

- The rich fool realized what was important after he died. Why? What did he finally understand?
- Why do you think Jesus said it was hard for the rich to enter the kingdom of God? How can things like greed and pride get in the way of your relationship with God?

Go Deeper

Read Psalm 24:1–2; 50:12; Jeremiah 9:23–26; Luke 16:1–18.

Prayer Starter

Think of what is important in your life, such as people's love and kindness. Thank God for everything He gives you and think of ways to use them to serve Him and help others.

Facts and Fun

How are elephants and camels similar? Jesus talked about how it was easier to get a camel through the eye of a needle than for a man in love with his money to get into heaven. The rabbis had a similar saying. They talked about getting "an elephant through a needle's eye."

Coming Up Next

Have you ever wanted to see something exciting but a big crowd was in the way? Next time, learn about two men who had to find a way around the crowds.

BESIDE THE ROAD AND UP A TREE

Some people will always find an excuse not to spend time with Jesus, but others won't let any obstacle get in their way! Read Luke 18:35–19:10 to meet two men who found a way to see Jesus!

Think About It

- It wasn't very dignified or "proper" for blind Bartimaeus to shout at Jesus, nor for rich Zacchaeus to climb a tree like a little kid! But they just didn't care. Why?
- Jesus wants you to know His love and be changed by it, just like the blind man and the tax collector. Have any of Jesus' words in the Bible changed you? How?

Go Deeper

Read Matthew 20:29–34; Mark 10:46–52; 2 Corinthians 5:17; Philippians 2:12–13.

Prayer Starter

Read Psalm 139:1–18 as a prayer today.

Facts and Fun

Zacchaeus the tax-collector was a real person. Ebenezer Scrooge was a fictional character. But what do they have in common?

(Answer: Both were rich misers who later changed and gave away a lot of their money to the poor.)

Coming Up Next

Most of the servants are heading for the bank, but one of them has a shovel and is heading for the backyard. What's up? Read all about it . . . next time!

THE MINA MYSTERY

The word "talent" is sometimes used for "mina." Both were money, but a "talent" can also be a God-given ability. Do you admire people who have many talents? Are you sometimes jealous of them? The Bible talks about talents and their use—read Luke 19:11–26.

Think About It

- Wisely investing and increasing money is very much like practicing something you're good at and getting even better at it. How are you "investing" *your* talents?
- Why do you think the master was so hard on the third servant? What kind of "help wanted" ad might he write to replace the servant who hid the mina?
- What talents or abilities has God given you? All talents can be used for God's work—how and where can you use yours?

Go Deeper

Read Luke 16:1–15; 1 Corinthians 7:7; 1 Peter 4:10.

Prayer Starter

Make a list of the talents and abilities God has given you and thank Him for them. Ask for God's help in using them with your family and friends, and at church.

Facts and Fun

In Jesus' time a mina was worth about three months' wages. Today that would be about $6,000.00.

Coming Up Next

Do you like to cheer and yell at ball games? Learn about a crowd that really had something to shout about . . . next time!

SHOUT IT OUT!

Has everyone gone crazy? They're shouting and hacking branches off trees and throwing their coats in the dust! Read Luke 19:28–48 to find out what's happening.

Think About It
- Jesus was like a king coming to be crowned. No wonder people were excited! How would you have felt if you were there?
- You don't have to worship only at church; the people in the story were outside. Where and when can you worship Jesus?

Go Deeper
Read Psalm 118:26; 150; Zechariah 9:9; Luke 20:1–47.

Prayer Starter
Read Mary's song in Luke 1:46–55 as a praise prayer. Think of all the great things God has done for you—especially sending Jesus as your Savior.

Facts and Fun
Imagine this scene as you come to your church to worship: The air is filled with loud noises as animals try to escape their cages or get loose. Sellers praise their animals and shout and cheat their customers, and buyers scream over the unfair prices. And oh, what a smell! It makes you think you are at a farmer's auction or in a barn. Not real inviting, is it?

Coming Up Next
Do you ever wish you could know the future? Learn about someone who told what the future would bring . . . next time!

I'M COMING BACK!

Would you like to know what's going to happen to you in the future? Jesus wanted the disciples to know that God knows the future and is always in control. Read Luke 21:5–28 to learn about the future.

Think About It

- Jesus told His disciples what would happen before His return. How can Jesus' words about the end times and His return affect the way you face problems now?
- What is happening today that makes the future look hopeless (for example, school shootings, famines)? When you feel like that, what can you do?

Go Deeper

Read Matthew 24:30; Mark 13:1–37; Luke 17:20–37; John 14:1–3; Revelation 1:7.

Prayer Starter

Tell God how you feel about the bad things happening around you. Then ask Him to help you be ready for His return. Thank God for preparing a place for you in heaven.

Facts and Fun

A nervous couple in California was so frightened by an earthquake that they sent their very active son to stay with relatives in Colorado. Two days later the relatives phoned saying, "We're sending your boy back. Send us the earthquake."

Coming Up Next

Have you ever been accused of something you didn't do, and it got people so mad at you they wanted to kill you? Read about a man this happened to . . . next time!

A DEADLY PLOT

Judas hurried down the street, clutching the silver coins. No one must know what he had done until . . . too late! What's happening? Read Luke 22:1–6; John 11:45–57; 12:20–28.

Think About It

- God used Judas's betrayal as part of His plan to save the world and you. Have you ever had bad things happen that later turned out for good? What?
- People who've been sick have more sympathy for others. People who've had to study hard learn good habits. What bad or hard things have taught you good lessons?

Go Deeper

Read Genesis 3:15; Isaiah 53:3–7; Luke 20:9–19; John 13:18–30.

Prayer Starter

Thank God that He knew from the beginning that Jesus would die for everyone's sins. Ask Him to show you how bad things that have happened to you actually had a good purpose.

Facts and Fun

Dad looked at Chad's drawing, an airplane with three passengers.

"Who are those people?" he asked.

"That's Mary, Joseph, and the baby Jesus," Chad replied. "They're running away from the bad king to Egypt."

"I didn't know they went by plane," said Dad.

Chad explained, "Oh yes! And Pontius the pilot is driving."

Coming Up Next

Ever play follow the leader? Learn new rules for the game . . . next time!

FOLLOW THE LEADER

Jesus had a towel wrapped around His waist. Did He just have a shower? Was He going swimming? Read Luke 22:13–23, 33–34; John 13:1–15 to find out what He was up to.

Think About It

- When Jesus gave the disciples their last supper together, He told them to "do this in remembrance of me." What does Jesus want you to remember?
- Jesus set an example by serving His disciples and washing their feet. How can you show love by serving others? (Setting the table, helping others with homework.)

Go Deeper

Read John 13:31–38; 14:1–31; Galatians 5:13; Philippians 2:1–5.

Prayer Starter

Print JESUS in the middle of a paper. Print words that tell how you can become like Jesus (loving, kind, serving) around His name. Thank God for Jesus' example and ask for guidance in following it.

Facts and Fun

Country roads in Jesus' day were very dusty, and animals used them. When people came into a house, they removed their sandals and had their feet washed. Washing a visitor's dirty, smelly feet was usually done by the lowest slave or servant.

Coming Up Next

What a night! Armies in the olive grove! Fishermen telling lies! False witnesses and bonfires! What's this all about? Find out . . . next time!

ARRESTED AND SENTENCED TO DEATH

"He's leading a rebellion! He's starting a tax revolt! He's dangerous! Kill Him!" Who is being talked about? Read Luke 22:47–71; John 18:23 to find out.

Think About It

- Why do you think Jesus was condemned for telling the truth?
- Have you ever been scared and acted like Peter? What happened? How did you feel afterward?
- Jesus never did anything wrong, yet He was falsely accused. How does that help you when people tell stories about you?

Go Deeper

Read Matthew 26:47–75; John 18:1–27; 2 Corinthians 5:21; Hebrews 4:14–15.

Prayer Starter

Tell God how it feels when others blame you for something you didn't do. He understands. After all, He went through it Himself.

Facts and Fun

Peter was very sorry that he had denied knowing Jesus. Figure out the secret message that tells what Peter did by writing the letter of the alphabet that comes after the one printed.

GD VDMS NTSRHCD ZMC VDOS AHSSDQKX.

Coming Up Next

What would you do to avoid being punished? Learn about someone who did nothing, even though that person was innocent . . . next time!

INNOCENT SUFFERER

Jesus was innocent and sinless and didn't deserve to be punished. He could stop this trial. Read John 18:28–19:12, 16 to see what He did.

Think About It

- Imagine you've been caught shoplifting and are about to be arrested. How would you feel if someone offered to take your punishment for you?
- Jesus' death paid for your sins. How does knowing that affect you?
- Jesus was beaten and whipped so badly He could hardly stand. Then He was nailed to a cross to die. He suffered all this because He loves you. How did His dying help you?

Go Deeper

Read Matthew 27:19–31; Luke 23:1–25; Romans 3:23; 6:23.

Prayer Starter

Read Isaiah 50:6–8 and think about Jesus' suffering for you. Thank Him for taking your place.

Facts and Fun

Pilate was a Roman governor in charge of Judea, where Jerusalem was located. The religious leaders hated Pilate because he had taken money from the temple treasuries to build a large system for carrying running water. Yet they became all buddy-buddy to Pilate when they wanted him to kill Jesus.

Coming Up Next

Black, black day! The sky is dark; soldiers stand on guard. The wicked are laughing and mocking. What's happening? Read all about it . . . next time!

DEAD AND BURIED

Imagine you are Jesus' close friend and now He is dead!
How do you feel? Read Luke 23:32–56 for the story.

Think About It

- Jesus' death happened at Passover, the celebration of when the lamb's blood on the doors saved the Israelite children from death in Egypt. How was Jesus like that spotless Passover lamb? Why was He the only one who could die for the sins of the world?

- Jesus showed love by dying for your sins. How can you return that love? (Be kind to others, read your Bible, etc.)

Go Deeper

Read Matthew 27:33–61; John 1:29; 19:1–42; 2 Corinthians 5:15–21.

Prayer Starter

If you've accepted that Jesus died to pay for your sins, God sees His blood on the "door" of your heart and passes over your sin to make you His child. Thank Jesus for this.

Facts and Fun

Jesus' tomb had a large stone in front of the opening. It was sealed by stretching a cord across the rock and putting a wax seal on the cord. The seal meant that, by the orders of the Roman government, no one was to disturb the tomb—and they could tell if anyone did by the broken seal.

Coming Up Next

How do you celebrate something that is so great you can hardly believe it? Learn how some reacted to an awesome event . . . next time!

THE VICTORY!

Satan probably thought he had won when Jesus died. He might even have done some devilish celebrating. But was *he* in for a surprise! Read John 20:1–21, 26–29 to discover the true winner.

Think About It

- Imagine how you would feel finding Jesus' tomb empty. What would your first thoughts be? Why? How easy would the truth be to believe?
- Jesus' defeat of sin, Satan, and eternal death is the most important thing that ever happened. Why is it so important? What difference does it make?

Go Deeper

Read Job 19:25–27; Luke 24:1–49; Acts 2:22–24, 32.

Prayer Starter

Sing or read a favorite Easter song as a prayer today.

Facts and Fun

The penalty for Roman soldiers sleeping on duty was death! But they were paid to say they'd fallen asleep and pretend Jesus' disciples had stolen His body. Strangely enough, they were not punished for falling asleep! Someone besides the disciples knew the truth. They wanted to hush it up. Nice try!

Coming Up Next

Now that Jesus conquered death and brought salvation, it's time to take action. What do you think the disciples did next? Find out . . . next time!

The book of Acts takes place in a very exciting time in history, when the Christian church was born. It was written by a doctor named Luke, who also wrote the Gospel of Luke. Travel with the first Christians to experience wonderful adventures filled with danger from enemies and storms, riots and imprisonments, and many glorious miracles. God's Holy Spirit gave these early believers the strength they needed to win over their enemies and spread the gospel of Christ.

A Special Gift

Listen as Jesus returns to heaven and tells His disciples to wait for a special gift. The Holy Spirit came on the day of Pentecost. Imagine the excitement as the Holy Spirit sweeps over the people and gives them power. The disciples boldly speak out about Christ, enduring beatings, prison, and sometimes death for their faith. A Jewish leader named Saul spent his time persecuting the church. But the Lord called Saul to follow Him, and he becomes a great missionary. The book of Acts records Saul's (called Paul) journeys telling others about Jesus. Luke often travels with Paul.

Why This Book

Luke wrote this book to show how the apostles, or "persons sent out on a mission," obeyed Jesus' orders to tell others about Him. It is the story of two leaders of the church, Peter and Paul. These men agreed that the Christian faith was not just for the Jews but for non-Jews as well.

Archaeologists Get In on the Act

Today, archaeologists have found items which have confirmed that Luke's story is true. Such places as the street in Damascus, "which is called Straight," where Paul went after his conversion, have been excavated. Archaeologists continue to dig up artifacts (objects made by a human) with names and dates that show that Luke was correct.

An Important Name

This book is often called "The Acts of the Apostles," but could also be referred to as "The Acts of the Holy Spirit." Be prepared to go on adventure after adventure as you read the wonderful acts of God in the lives of the first Christians.

OH, AND ONE LAST THING!

The last thing that someone tells you is usually something they want you to remember. Read John 14:1–3; Acts 1:1–26 to learn what Jesus' important final commands were before going to heaven.

Think About It

- After Jesus blessed His disciples, He rose (ascended) into heaven. What kind of celebration do you think there was when He arrived in heaven?
- The Bible says that Jesus "sits at the right hand of God." How does it make you feel to know that Jesus is next to God watching over you?

Go Deeper

Read Hebrews 8:1–2; 9:24–25; 10:12–14 to learn more about Jesus in heaven. Read Mark 16:15–16; Luke 24:50–53; 1 Thessalonians 4:13–18.

Prayer Starter

Think about it! Jesus is in heaven today, alive and watching over you! Think of someone you could tell about Jesus. Ask God to help you talk about Jesus' birth, death, resurrection, and return to heaven.

Facts and Fun

Heavenly Trivia

Jesus said to enter the kingdom of heaven, we must become like what? *(Answer: A little child)*

Where did Jesus say we should store up our treasures? *(Answer: Heaven)*

Who said, "In my Father's house are many rooms"? *(Answer: Jesus)*

Coming Up Next

Did you ever want to speak in a different language? Learn how God helped some people do just that . . . next time!

FIRE AND WIND

When Jesus left, He told His followers that He would not leave them alone. What did He mean? Who would He send to help? Read Acts 2:1–21, 37–42 for the answer.

Think About It

- Jews who lived in many faraway countries and spoke many different languages had come to Jerusalem to celebrate Pentecost. How did God show them He cared about them?
- How can learning someone's language show them that *you* love them? Once God got the people's attention, what did Peter do? Did it work?

Go Deeper

Read Matthew 3:11; John 16:7, 13–15; 1 Corinthians 12:13.

Prayer Starter

Thank the Lord for sending His Spirit to help and guide you. Tell Him if you want His Spirit to work in your life and heart. Ask God to show you how He does that.

Facts and Fun

Father: "Well! That's a change! Normally you talk on the phone for hours! This time you only talked half an hour. How come?"

Daughter: "It was the wrong number."

Coming Up Next

Not everyone wanted to believe in Jesus. Next time read about the problems the disciples faced.

TROUBLE IN JERUSALEM

Ever been in a situation where you were told not to tell the truth? Learn what happened when the disciples were forbidden to tell the truth. It's in Acts 3:1–13, 16; 4:1, 18–31.

Think About It

- When the priests and religious rulers ordered the apostles not to witness about Jesus, what did the apostles do? Why? Have you ever been in a situation like this? What did you do?
- Have you ever prayed for God to change kids who didn't like you? What happened?

Go Deeper

Read John 15:18–27; Acts 3:17–26; 4:4–20; 2 Timothy 3:12; 1 Peter 1:6–9.

Prayer Starter

Think about a time when you were afraid to speak boldly about your faith in Jesus. Tell God honestly how you felt. How could you have responded differently? If the disciples' prayer in Acts 4:24–26, 29–30 is what you want, pray it today.

Facts and Fun

Pretend to be a TV interviewer getting the big story on the latest happenings in Jerusalem. Think of some questions that you would want to ask Peter, John, or the beggar. How might they answer according to today's reading? What might be the reaction of the average person on the street?

Coming Up Next

You would think miracles would help people believe in Jesus. They often do, but not always! Find out what happened when the disciples worked miracles . . . next time!

MORE MIRACLES, MORE TROUBLE

Did persecution stop the disciples? No way! Read Acts 5:12–42 to find out how they kept going and what happened.

Think About It

- Being imprisoned and beaten did not stop the apostles from sharing Christ. What kinds of problems might keep you from sharing your faith in Jesus?
- Gamaliel said that the Sanhedrin might be fighting against God, and he was right. How does it help to know that God is on your side and your enemies are really fighting Him?

Go Deeper

Read Acts 1:8; 8:4–8, 26–40; 2 Corinthians 4:8–15; 1 Peter 4:16.

Prayer Starter

Persecution is no fun, whether kids call you names, laugh at you, or try to hurt you. Tell God what makes it hard for you to share your beliefs. Pray for courage and wisdom. Thank God for His miracles that prove that Jesus is His Son.

Facts and Fun

Did you know that "flogging" was beating a person with a stick or a whip? Often the whip was made of several leather strips with pieces of sharp metal, rock, or bone at the ends. Ouch! The rocks and metal would leave cuts on the person's back, making permanent scars.

Coming Up Next

Standing up for Jesus can be scary. Find out how one man stood his ground . . . next time!

STANDING FOR THE TRUTH

Has anyone picked on you because you are a Christian? Read about a man who stood up for Christ even when his enemies picked up stones in Acts 6:8–15; 7:1, 51–60.

Think About It

- A Christian martyr speaks boldly about Jesus but is persecuted, or killed, for his or her faith. How did Stephen fit this description?
- Stephen's belief that Jesus is the Christ and his love for God gave him strength to speak boldly. When have you told others about Jesus?

Go Deeper

Read Psalm 42:10–11; Acts 6:1–7; 7:1–50; Colossians 4:3–6; 2 Timothy 4:2.

Prayer Starter

Decide how you would like to tell people the truth about Jesus (for example, when they ask why you go to church, why you believe God created everything, etc.). Pray for the opportunity to speak the truth and help to stand firm when someone asks about or makes fun of your faith.

Facts and Fun

Today there are a lot of Christians in countries such as China, India, or Iran, where Christianity is not accepted. Ask a grown-up to help you find out about some of these people. Pray for them or write to them and encourage them.

Coming Up Next

Have you known anyone who changed after accepting Jesus? Meet a man who even changed his name . . . next time!

BIG CHANGES

Saul is hunting down Christians, beating them, locking them in prison, shouting for them to die! Now *he* would make a good apostle, right? Read Acts 8:1–3; 9:1–19 for the shocking answer.

Think About It

- Saul spent his entire time trying to destroy the church. Why do you think Saul felt he was doing the right thing? What kinds of things might he have thought to himself?
- Has God ever wanted you to do something loving for a bully who picks on Christians? What did you do?

Go Deeper

Read Psalm 111:10; Proverbs 19:2–3; John 14:6; Acts 9:20–31.

Prayer Starter

Is there one thing in your life that your parents tell you to do that you just don't want to do, or something Jesus said that is hard for you to obey? Pray about it and ask God to help you change.

Facts and Fun

Atheists are people who don't believe in God. One day a young boy asked his atheist parents, "Do you think God knows that we don't believe in Him?"

Coming Up Next

The man standing on the roof was so hungry he could've eaten almost anything! But when he saw what was on the menu, he changed his mind. Read about it . . . next time!

REPTILES IN THE BEDSHEET

Peter was staying with Simon, the tanner. Tanners cleaned animal hides to make leather, and their houses *stank!* But Peter had some attitudes that were even stinkier! Read Acts 10:9–28, 34–48.

Think About It

- Jews considered non-Jews unclean and sinful because they worshiped other gods, so Jews had nothing to do with them. What was God telling Peter?
- Why was this hard to accept? Is there anyone whom you find difficult to accept?

Go Deeper

Read Acts 10:1–8; 11:1–26; Galatians 3:28; 2 Peter 3:9.

Prayer Starter

Is there anyone you look down upon? Honestly tell God how you feel. Ask Jesus to show you that He loves all people and to help you do the same.

Facts and Fun

Pour salt and sugar on a plate. Spin the plate around. Can you tell which is which? Like sugar and salt, outwardly people all look pretty much the same. But it's our "taste" or our hearts that count. Peter had to learn that God sees the heart and all that matters is that a person believes in Him.

Coming Up Next

Have you ever been in a bad situation and thought there was no way out? Find out next time about when Peter was in just such a predicament.

PRISON BREAK!

Has God ever done anything truly astonishing in your life? What happened? Read Acts 12:1–25 to learn about a time that God did something fantastic for Peter.

Think About It

- The same religious leaders who had beaten and killed Jesus now had Peter in prison. What do you think he expected them to do to him?
- Why do you think Peter thought he saw a vision?
- Have you ever had something happen that was so good you could hardly believe it? What?

Go Deeper

Read Psalm 77:13; Isaiah 55:9; John 21:18–19, 21–23; Romans 12:2; Hebrews 11:36.

Prayer Starter

Prayer isn't getting God to do what you want, but lining up your heart with God's will. So pray that God will help you to want the same things He wants.

Facts and Fun

Ever get confused by all the Herods in the Bible?

Herod the Great reigned when Jesus was born. He met the wise men and killed the baby boys (Matthew 2:16).

Herod Antipas, Herod the Great's son, beheaded John the Baptist (Matthew 14:3–10).

Herod Agrippa, Herod Antipas' nephew, ruled during Acts. He killed James, but died soon after (Acts 12:1–4). Great family—not!

Coming Up Next

Next time, read how the Holy Spirit picked out two men and told them to hit the road!

SPECIAL SERVICE

Paul has a run-in with a sorcerer, and they clash right in the governor's palace! Suddenly one of them is struck blind! Who wins this battle? Read Acts 13:1–15, 42–52 to find out!

Think About It

- How do you think Paul and Barnabas felt when they were told to head out from Antioch to preach the gospel (the good news about Jesus) in new lands?
- You may not know what special job God has planned for your life, but what could you do for God right now?

Go Deeper

Read Matthew 28:18–20; Acts 13:16–41; 14:1–28; Colossians 3:23–24. (Think of how Paul and Barnabas fulfilled Jesus' "Great Commission" in Matthew.)

Prayer Starter

Be quiet for a few minutes. Imagine what it was like for Paul and Barnabas. Talk to God about how you can be a missionary like them in your everyday life.

Facts and Fun

Up until this battle in the governor's palace, Luke always mentioned Barnabas' name before Paul's. But at this point, Paul became the leader and from now on, his name was mentioned first.

Coming Up Next

It was the first major disagreement in the church, and it was a *big* one! Find out how it came to an end . . . next time!

SOMETHING SOUR TURNS SWEET

"To be a Christian you have to do *what?* I don't think so!" What's the apostle Paul getting so steamed about? Read Acts 15:1–12, 22–31 to find out.

Think About It
- Paul didn't want to argue with other Christians, but he did need to stand up for the truth. How do *you* react when someone says something untrue?
- It is important to discuss disagreements so everyone understands what each is saying. Have you ever resolved an argument with someone by talking things out?

Go Deeper
Read Genesis 50:20; Jeremiah 29:11; Luke 11:46; Acts 15:13–21; Romans 8:28.

Prayer Starter
Thank God for being able to make good come out of an argument or bad situation. Explain some things in your life that you would like Him to turn around for good.

Facts and Fun
Only Jews could pass beyond the outer courtyard of the temple, or the Court of Gentiles. Warning signs were posted forbidding entry on the threat of death. Some Jews nearly rioted when they thought Paul had taken Greek friends into the inner courtyards. Is it any wonder that such ideas about the Gentiles carried over into the Christian church?

Coming Up Next
Do you think you would rejoice if you were thrown into prison because of your faith? Learn about some men who did . . . next time!

RELATIONSHIPS/SALVATION

PRAISES IN PRISON

Have you ever had a day when everything seemed to go wrong? Did you grumble or stay happy anyway? How did your attitude affect those around you? To find out what Paul and Silas did on a really bad day, read Acts 16:16–40.

Think About It
- What reasons did Paul and Silas have to sing in prison? Who did they put their trust in?
- Do you think the jailer was surprised to hear Paul and Silas praising God? What might have influenced the jailer to believe in Christ?
- What situations would you find hard to rejoice in (when your team loses, when kids tease you for being a Christian)?

Go Deeper
Read more about Paul and Silas in Acts 17:1–18:23; 2 Corinthians 4:7–8; 11:24–27. Read Philippians 2:14–16; 4:4–7; 1 Thessalonians 5:18.

Prayer Starter
What's your biggest problem right now? Try thanking and praising God. Ask for help to be thankful for problems and trials. Think about those around you who you might influence with your good attitude.

Facts and Fun
Why do they say "Amen" at the end of a prayer instead of "A women"?
(Answer: The same reason they sing Hymns instead of Hers!)

Coming Up Next
Christians burning books worth nearly $500,000? What's happening? Next time, find out why sorcerers decided to torch their libraries!

HOT TIME IN THE OLD TOWN!

What happens when people meet the true God? They change! The old junk has to go! Read Acts 19:1, 8–20, 23–29, 35–41 to find out how a whole city changed.

Think About It

- Paul showed God's power through miracles. Why were the sons of Sceva unable to cast out demons?
- Games, books, or music might get in the way of living for God. Do you think you should talk to a parent or pastor about those things? Why?

Go Deeper

Read Acts 17:24–25; 18:24–19:7; 20:1–38 to learn about other cities that heard the Good News.

Prayer Starter

Ask Jesus to show you anything that keeps you from honoring Him. Pray and ask Him if there is anything wrong or evil in your room or life that He wants you to get rid of.

Facts and Fun

Did you know that Diana's temple in Ephesus was one of the Seven Wonders of the World? It was built of white marble and overlaid with gold, silver, and jewels. But within a few years so many people of Ephesus had become Christians that the pagan temples were nearly empty.

Coming Up Next

The mob was so insanely mad at Paul that they were screaming as they tried to beat him to death! Next time, find out if Paul survived!

GOD'S PROTECTION

Paul just never seemed to be able to stay out of trouble!
Read Acts 21:15–17, 26–36; 23:12–17, 23–24 to see how
Paul's enemies kept trying to kill him.

Think About It

- Although Paul was pretty sure that he might go to
  prison, why did he have the confidence to go to
  Jerusalem?
- God protected Paul because He wanted to use him to
  preach the gospel. Think of times God has protected
  you. What are you willing to do with your life to
  honor God?

Go Deeper

Read Psalm 116:6–7; Proverbs 2:7–8; Acts 21:1–25,
37–23:11, 18–35.

Prayer Starter

Decide if you would be willing to do anything or go
anywhere for Jesus. If you would, then tell God. Ask Him to
protect you so that, like Paul, you can tell others about Jesus.

Facts and Fun

Most people in the Roman Empire were slaves. Very few
were citizens. Roman citizens had special privileges: They
had the right to travel anywhere in the empire; they could
appeal to Roman courts. While a noncitizen would be
whipped if accused of serious crimes, it was against the law
to even tie the hands of a Roman citizen!

Coming Up Next

Have you ever thought that you should have told
somebody about Jesus, but it was too late? Find out how
Paul constantly shared Jesus . . . next time!

GOD PROTECTS/WITNESSING

JUMP AT THE CHANCE

Remember a time when you stood before somebody important like a principal or police officer? What thoughts went through your head? Read Acts 24:1–27 to find out how Paul made the best of his chances.

Think About It

- What was Paul's main goal—to be freed or to share the good news about Jesus? How would things have been different if Paul had fought to keep from going to prison?
- Think of some times you may have the chance to tell others about Jesus. What things do you worry about? How do you think God could take care of your worries?

Go Deeper

Read Acts 25:1–26:32 to find out about other chances Paul had to share the gospel. Read Matthew 10:19; Ephesians 5:15–16; 1 Peter 3:15; 4:11.

Prayer Starter

Ask God to give you courage and boldness even before important people.

Facts and Fun

Felix's conscience bothered him, so when Paul spoke about how God would judge sin, he was afraid. Nevertheless, he kept hoping that Paul would give him a bribe. Many people are only interested in Christianity for what they think they can get out of it.

Coming Up Next

Ever wonder what it would be like to be shipwrecked and thrown into the raging sea? Find out what happened to Paul when his ship crashed . . . next time!

SHIPWRECKED ADVENTURE

Day after day, the sky was ink black! No sun, no stars, just a howling, raging storm! No wonder everyone gave up hope! Read Acts 27:1–2, 6–27, 39–44 to discover the ship's final, fearful fate.

Think About It

- In the middle of the terrible, raging storm, Paul calmly said no one would be lost or drowned. How could he say that?
- At first the sailors and other prisoners thought Paul was crazy, but after everything he said came true, what might they have thought about his God?
- What "lifeboats," like good grades or good looks, do you hang on to in your life that you think will help you succeed?

Go Deeper

Read Acts 27:28–38. Read Acts 28 to find out what happened on shore. Read Proverbs 3:5–6; John 14:1.

Prayer Starter

Think of the most dangerous thing you have had to face. Tell God how you feel during hard times. Ask for help to trust in Him during such dangers.

Facts and Fun

Did you know that Paul was the first surfer in the Bible? *(Answer: At Malta he came ashore on a board!)*

Coming Up Next

Rome was a huge city of idol worshippers, made rich by oppressing the poor and exploiting the slaves. Why would God send Paul there? Find out . . . next time!

ROMANS

Have you ever received a letter from someone you've never met? Well, you're about to!

Paul's travels took him to some of the most exciting cities in Asia and Europe. Everywhere he went he started Christian churches. The book of Romans is an epistle or letter. Paul wrote it to the Christians in Rome five or six years before he was taken there as a prisoner. He had heard of their strong belief in Christ and was anxious to meet them. Historians believe that the church in Rome was started by Jews who were at Pentecost and then returned home. Paul had never been to Rome, but he planned to visit and wanted to introduce himself to the church before he arrived.

The Capital of the World

Rome was the busiest city in the world at that time and was the capital of the known world. It was twelve miles wide and built on seven low, flat hills east of the Tiber River. About 20,000 Jews lived in Rome, but the emperor, Claudius, drove them out of the city. Later, Christians in Rome were persecuted too. Nero was the Roman emperor when Paul wrote his letter in A.D. 57. He was considered one of the cruelest of all the emperors and the first to persecute Christians. Jews and Christians dug out tunnels and rooms under the city and out in the country. Imagine yourself in a Christian meeting to worship in these rooms and passages called "catacombs." Over 600 miles of catacombs still run under the city of Rome today!

Good News

Paul explains in his letter that everyone has sinned because we are all descendants or "children" of Adam. He tells of God's big plan and the good news that Jesus Christ died to take away our sins. Paul encourages the believers by telling them that God loves them and is willing to forgive them. This letter holds up Abraham as an example of faith. Abraham did many great things, but his faith pleased God the most. Paul asks the Romans, "How can a sinful person ever be good enough to be acceptable to a holy God?" Simple. By faith in Christ and acceptance of His death for our sins. Listen intently with the Romans to find out how to discover God's will and how to live the Christian life.

THE REAL THING

Have you ever wondered why there are so many bad things in this world? Read Romans 1:18–32; 2:1–4 to find out how God feels about sin and wickedness.

Think About It

- Paul said that nature—the things God created—shows us that God is real and powerful. What in nature shows you that God is real?
- Look at the sins listed in Romans 1:29–31. Have you ever been guilty of any of those? Which ones? What were the results?

Go Deeper

Read Romans 1:1–17, then continue on in Romans 2:5–3:8 to learn about God's faithfulness. Read Isaiah 40:28; Hebrews 11:3, 6.

Prayer Starter

Take a prayer walk in the park. Use all your senses—smell, taste, touch, hearing, sight—to soak in God's goodness. Thank God for the beauty of His creation.

Facts and Fun

The fish was an early symbol of Christianity. The Greek word for fish, *ichthus*, is an acronym, with the first letter (or letters) of each word in the phrase *Iesous Christos Theou Huios Soteros*, which means "Jesus Christ, of God the Son, Savior." It was used as a secret password between Christians persecuted by the Romans.

Coming Up Next

Do you ever think it is too hard to be good? Find out next time that no one can ever be good enough. That's why we need God!

SLAVE, CHOOSE YOUR MASTER!

Did you know you're a slave? Surprise! Read about it in Romans 3:20–31; 6:15–23 and find out how to choose your "master" and become "righteous" (good).

Think About It
- Romans tells us that we have all sinned and deserve to die. But God made a plan for Jesus to save us. How does that make you feel?
- If we keep on sinning, we earn death. What gift is better than those awful wages? How do we get that gift?

Go Deeper
Read Matthew 19:17; Romans 4–6:14; 2 Peter 3:9.

Prayer Starter
Just think, God loves you so much that He sent Jesus to save you and forgive your sin. Without Jesus, you're a "slave to sin." Ask God to help you learn how to become a "slave to righteousness."

Facts and Fun
In Paul's time, Rome's population was about one million people—and most were slaves! In the Roman Colosseum, gladiators fought and killed each other. Later, Christians were killed by animals or gladiators for sport. In Rome, people were not valued very much, but Paul wrote a letter telling these people how much God loved them.

Coming Up Next
The coolest friends! The hottest computer games! The best toys! The most expensive clothes! Is this what we should *live* for? Learn a better way . . . next time!

GOD'S GRACE/JESUS SAVES US

I DON'T WANT TO!

You probably think it's easy to do what you want. Think again! If what you want is to live God's way, it's a struggle. Read Romans 7:4–6, 14–20, 24–25; 8:5–14; 13:8, 10–14.

Think About It

- Paul says in his struggle with sin that he didn't want to do the things he did. What things do you find yourself doing that you do not want to do?
- Paul said, "Don't think about how to gratify (satisfy) the desires of the sinful nature." What are some bad desires you shouldn't even think about trying to satisfy (such as stealing cool toys or watching forbidden movies)? What should you think about instead?

Go Deeper

Read John 14:23; Romans 7:1–3, 7–13; 8:1–4, 15–39; 12:1–13:14; 1 Corinthians 13:3–8; Galatians 2:20.

Prayer Starter

Do you sometimes find it hard to live the Christian life? Honestly admit it to God. Thank Him for the good things that happen when you follow His way.

Facts and Fun

A student answered a test question by writing, "Only God knows the answer to this question." The teacher responded, "God gets an A. You get an F." Fortunately, however, God has written the answers to life's most important questions in the Bible! Read it and find out how to live!

Coming Up Next

Find out the most important thing Jesus came to teach us . . . next time!

I'M ALLOWED BUT I WON'T

Have you ever done something that you knew was okay, but might make someone else question why you did it? Read Romans 14:1–19; 15:1–7 to find out how to deal with life's "gray area" issues.

Think About It

- Think of a time when someone acted like they were more important than you or judged you wrongly. How did you feel? How do you think God feels about that?
- What kinds of things should we and can we do to encourage others to obey Jesus?
- List some things you could do to show others that you love them. How can your attitude be more like Jesus'?

Go Deeper

Read Mark 10:31; Romans 14:20–23; 15:8–13; Philippians 2:3–8; 1 John 4:7.

Prayer Starter

Ask God to show you how you might be upsetting others by the things you do, accidentally turning them away from God instead of toward Him. Ask Him to help you think of others before yourself. Take a few minutes to think of specific ways you can do this—such as the movies you watch, jokes you tell, etc.

Facts and Fun

A little boy's prayer: "Dear God, take care of Mommy, Daddy, Grandpa, and Grandma, but most of all take care of Yourself. 'Cause if anything happens to You, we would all be in a terrible mess!"

Creative Ideas for Times with God

When you have a really good friend, you like to spend time together, right? Well, that's what quiet times are—spending time with God. He wants to be your best friend. Sometimes with a friend you talk and share your feelings. Sometimes you both spend time with other people. Other times you are just quiet, and being alone together is enough.

The Bible tells us that we can "pray continually" (1 Thessalonians 5:17). That means that you can talk to God all the time—anywhere and any place. You have no other friend that you can talk to *all the time*. Here are some ideas on how you can spend your time with God.

1. Start a prayer reminder basket or box. Put things in the box that remind you of God's creation, like rocks, seashells, or pinecones. Put in pictures of friends or family or small items that remind you of them. Add newspaper clippings of things happening in your community or the world. During your quiet time reach into the box and pull out one item. Talk to God about what comes to your mind when you see this thing.

2. In Matthew 6:6, Jesus tells His disciples to go into their rooms, close the doors, and pray to their Father in heaven. Some versions of the Bible say "closet" instead of room. Clear a place on the floor in your closet. Take a flashlight with you and close the door. Spend some time talking to God, or just enjoy being alone with Him.

3. After asking permission, take a walk around your neighborhood. Walk slowly. As you pass by houses where your friends live, talk to God about them. If you pass your school, pray for the teachers and staff who work there. Ask God to show you how you can pray for your community.

4. Make a "prayer list" of people or things you want to remember to talk to God about. You can write this list or draw pictures. You could paste pictures of people you want to pray about on poster board and keep it near where you have your quiet time.

5. Here's an activity to help you watch your faith grow. Wad up a paper towel, preferably a colored one, and stuff it into a plastic or Styrofoam™ cup. Push two bean seeds halfway down the inside of the cup, between the cup and the towel. Pour enough water to dampen the towel but not soak it. Place the cup by a sunny window. Watch the seeds sprout and grow as your faith in God grows! Your daily readings are like the roots of the plant, and your prayers are the leaves shooting up to God.

6. Even when you know that God is there, it sometimes can be hard to talk to someone you cannot see. Write your prayers as if you were writing a letter to God. You can even draw a picture expressing your feelings to God.

7. Take a blanket outside, lay down, and watch the clouds roll by. Ask a friend to join you. Talk about what the shapes of the clouds remind you of. Share with each other how you feel about God's love, peace, and goodness, or even about the funny animals God made that show His sense of humor.

8. Talk some friends into putting on a Bible skit. Dig out old robes, blankets, towels, etc., to make costumes. Assign characters and write dialogue. Record a video or put on a skit for other friends or families.

9. Listen to different types of music such as classical, hymns, Christian pop, or Christian rap. Think about how each type of music makes you think of a different part of God's personality.

10. Who is your favorite Bible character? Become that character for a day. Imagine that you're a slave like Joseph—or become a giant slayer like David. Ask your family to call you by that name for the day—Joseph, David, or Moses. Think about how God used that person to do great things for Him, and how He can use you.

11. Throw a Bible-character party. (Check with your parents first.) Write the description of different characters on each invitation and the book, chapter, and verse of the Bible that talks about that character. The guests should dress up like they think that character looked. At the party the guests have to ask each other questions to guess which character they are.

12. Set your alarm to go off before the sun rises. Go outside and spend some time alone with God as the sun comes up. Think about this passage: Isaiah 50:4, "The Sovereign LORD has given me an instructed tongue, to know the word that sustains the weary. He wakens me morning by morning, wakens my ear to listen like one being taught."

13. Rent one of the old classic movies based on the Bible, like *Ben Hur* or *The Robe*. Pretend you are a movie critic. Look up the story in the Bible before you watch it and again after to see how close the writers came to the true story. Give a review on the good and the bad of the movie.

14. Turn off all the lights at night and light only a candle. Think about the passage Matthew 5:14–16, "You are the light of the world. A city on a hill cannot be hidden. Neither do people light a lamp and put it under a bowl. Instead they put it on its stand, and it gives light to everyone in the house. In the same way, let your light shine before men, that they may see your good deeds and praise your Father in heaven." Think about how you can let your light shine.

Radical Places to Have a Quiet Time

Here are some places where you can have your quiet time:

- On a porch swing
- On the beach
- Riding a bike
- Sitting under a tree
- Sitting on the back steps of your house
- In a tent in your backyard
- Behind the family-room couch
- In the back seat of your car
- Beside a lake
- On a skateboard
- Under your bed
- In a tree house
- Sitting in a garden
- Under the kitchen table
- Walking on a hiking trail
- On the swings in your school yard
- Sitting on a park bench
- On top of a high hill or mountain
- In the shower or bathtub
- Under the stars
- Anywhere you think you can be alone with God!

Suggestions for Extra Things to Do During Your Times with God

Ever have those days where you just want more? Well, here are some ideas for things you can do to beef up or pack more into your quiet times.

- The book of Proverbs has 31 chapters. Read a chapter a day, matching each day of the month. For example, on the 15th of the month, read Proverbs 15. If you skip a day, just pick up with the chapter matching that date.

- Read a Psalm a day until you read through the book of Psalms. (This will take you half a year!!)

- Read one chapter of Acts a day until you read through the whole book.

- Read one chapter of Romans a day until you read

through the whole book.

- Read through a modern English version of *Pilgrim's Progress*. This is a great book by John Bunyan about the Christian life. It's full of adventure, choices, villains, and heroes—and *strange* happenings!

- Read the *Chronicles of Narnia* books by C. S. Lewis. If you've never read them, GET THEM! They're fantastic!

- Watch videos like *Veggie Tales* or *Adventures in Odyssey*, and instead of just enjoying them, think about what spiritual principles they teach.

- Listen to soft, instrumental guitar music while you read your Bible.

- Read the *Adventure Bible Handbook*, two to three pages a day. This book takes you on an amazing adventure through the Bible, giving you all kinds of fascinating, amusing, and exciting facts.

- Read the *Amazing Treasure Bible Storybook*, four to five pages a day. Solve clues from reading Bible stories and move from room to room in an ancient Middle Eastern castle.

- Memorize a Bible verse every day.

- Make up a tune for a Psalm, or two, and sing it. The tune doesn't need to be fancy. Make it catchy or give it a tune that matches the words—sad with a sad tune, joyful with something really fun, and so on.

- Read gospel stories out loud, dramatizing the voices of each speaker and making sound effects when action happens.

- After reading a chapter in your Bible, read the same story in another translation to help you get a clearer picture of what happened.

- Before you read from a book of the Bible, read the comments on that book in the *Adventure Bible Handbook*.

Now you think of some creative ways to have a quiet time!

An Index of Exciting Reads!

God Does the Impossible!—and Really Cool Stuff!

Shepherd Clobbers Robber Kings!
Genesis 14:1-24

Wanderers, Women, and Wells
Genesis 24:1-4, 10-27; 26:12-25, 32; 29:1-12; Exodus 2:11-21;
John 4:1-15

Good Snake Exposes Magicians!
Exodus 4:1-5, 29-31; 7:7-12; 2 Timothy 3:8-9

Ice from Heaven's Freezer
Exodus 9:13-26; Joshua 10:6-11; Psalm 18:12-14; Revelation 8:6-7;
16:17-21

Who Needs a Bridge?
Exodus 14:15-22; Joshua 3:9-17; 2 Kings 2:5-14

Manna: Bread from Heaven
Exodus 16:1-15; Psalm 78:23-25; John 6:5-13, 25-35

Giants!—Anakites & Rephaites
Numbers 13:21-33; Deuteronomy 2:18-21; 3:3-11; Joshua 15:13-14;
1 Samuel 17:1-8, 48-49; 2 Samuel 21:15-22

Help Us Hide Out!
Joshua 2:1-7; 2 Samuel 17:15-21; 1 Kings 18:1-4; Jeremiah 36:25-26

Deborah and Other Wise Women
Judges 4:1-22; 13:1-24; 2 Kings 11:1-3; 2 Chronicles 34:14-28;
Daniel 5:5-12

Philistines: Friends or Foes?
1 Samuel 18:5-16; 21:10-22:1; 27:1-6; 29:1-7; 2 Samuel 5:17-25;
8:1

Priest Joins Band of Outlaws!
1 Samuel 21:1-9; 22:6-23

Riffraff and Mighty Men
1 Samuel 22:1-2; 27:1-2; 2 Samuel 21:15-22; 23:8-23

I Coulda Done You In!
1 Samuel 24:1-22; 26:1-25; 31:1-6; 2 Samuel 5:1-3

Wise Wife, Foolish Husband
1 Samuel 25:1-44

Lion Kills Prophet, Spares Donkey!
1 Kings 12:25–13:34

They Came Back for More!
1 Kings 17:17–24; 2 Kings 4:17–37; 13:20–21; Matthew 9:18–26;
27:50–53; Luke 7:11–17; John 11:17, 32–44;
Acts 9:36–42; 20:7–12

Beat-up Prophet Warns Ahab!
1 Kings 20:1–43

Speedy Jehu Fools Baal's Boys!
2 Kings 9:1–28; 10:17–27

Plague Angel Reveals Temple Site!
1 Chronicles 21:1–22:1

Can't Keep a Good Man Down!
Job 1:1–2:13; 42:1–17; James 5:10–11

You Don't Give Up, Do You?
Matthew 15:21–28; 20:29–34; Luke 11:5–10; 18:1–8

John the Baptist—the Waterboy
Matthew 14:1–12; Luke 3:1–22; 7:18–35; John 1:15–34

Son of God Defies Gravity!
Luke 24:50–51; John 6:16–20; Acts 1:6–9

Angels and Earthquakes
Acts 5:17–24; 12:1–11; 16:22–34

Evangelist Driven Out of Town!
Acts 9:23–30; 13:49–51; 16:35–40; 17:5–14

Apostle Attacked and Beaten!
Acts 14:19–20; 16:16–23; 18:12–13; 21:27–32; 2 Corinthians
11:23–26

Shipwrecked Again and Again!
Acts 27:9–44; 2 Corinthians 11:25

Kids! Don't You Try This!
Numbers 21:4–9; Isaiah 11:8–9; Mark 16:17–18; Acts 28:1–6

Reading by the Book

Genesis
17–36, 42, 96, 162, 180

Exodus
29, 39–51, 54, 55, 84, 87,
102, 104, 118, 135, 148

Leviticus
50

Numbers
45, 50, 52–57

Deuteronomy
23, 47, 48, 49, 54, 57, 58–59,
65, 71, 77, 85, 86, 104, 110,
115, 135, 148

Joshua
27, 56, 57, 63–67, 117, 118,
125

Judges
59, 71–74

Ruth
77

1 Samuel
25, 30, 73, 81–92, 137

2 Samuel
64, 90, 92, 93–97

1 Kings
82, 94, 96, 101–108, 113

2 Kings
85, 109–119

1 Chronicles
67, 92, 94, 95, 124

2 Chronicles
48, 103, 123

Ezra
123–125

Nehemiah
104, 126

Esther
129–130

Job
17, 85, 167

Psalms
18, 27, 28, 29, 31, 33, 35, 39,
41, 43, 44, 45, 49, 51, 52, 53,
54, 56, 64, 65, 66, 71, 73, 82,
83, 84, 85, 86, 88, 89, 92, 93,
94, 97, 107, 111, 112, 115, 117,
118, 124, 125, 126, 129, 130,
135, 137, 145, 148, 150, 151,
156, 157, 158, 160, 175, 176,
178, 183

Proverbs
22, 34, 43, 52, 59, 64, 67, 72,
77, 88, 91, 92, 107, 116, 119,
129, 135, 145, 176, 183, 185

Ecclesiastes
123, 126

Isaiah
17, 23, 25, 53, 56, 82, 83, 102,
113, 117, 119, 123, 134, 144,
151, 162, 165, 178, 189

Jeremiah
22, 28, 31, 35, 106, 115, 116,
117, 118, 119, 157, 180

Ezekiel
150

Hosea
115, 155

Micah
94, 134

Haggai
124

Zechariah
160

Malachi
109

Matthew
33, 39, 40, 47, 54, 57, 58, 77,
89, 95, 96, 105, 106, 109, 110,
134, 136, 139, 143, 146, 147,
148, 152, 154, 155, 158, 161,
164, 165, 166, 172, 179, 184,
190

Mark
18, 51, 101, 104, 113, 138, 146,
149, 152, 153, 155, 158, 161,
171, 192

Luke
22, 29, 36, 40, 49, 51, 66, 81,
106, 109, 111, **133–139,** 141,
142, 143, **144–147,** 149, 150,
152, 153, **154–164, 166** 167,
171, 180

John
19, 24, 30, 33, 42, 44, 45, 46,
55, 57, 58, 65, 82, 93, 101, 111,
133, **140–141,** 142, **143,** 144,
147, **148–151, 153,** 161, **162–
165,** 166, **167, 171,** 172, 173,
176, 178, 185, 191

Acts
25, 35, 36, 39, 40, 67, 84, 87,
93, 102, 108, 111, 115, 138,
141, 167, **171–185**

Romans
18, 19, 23, 27, 28, 31, 41, 47,
67, 84, 91, 104, 110, 114, 140,
165, 178, 180, **189–192**

1 Corinthians
18, 32, 34, 42, 44, 49, 52, 54,
55, 67, 71, 74, 77, 90, 96, 103,
136, 139, 151, 159, 172, 191

2 Corinthians
50, 59, 65, 73, 81, 95, 97, 140,
158, 164, 166, 174, 181

Galatians
108, 113, 151, 163, 177, 191

Ephesians
20, 55, 63, 147, 156, 184

Philippians
20, 21, 26, 91, 94, 110, 153,
158, 163, 181, 192

Colossians
66, 83, 113, 123, 175, 179

1 Thessalonians
72, 103, 171, 181

1 Timothy
41, 86, 102

2 Timothy
32, 46, 103, 114, 118, 139,
173, 175

Titus
34

Hebrews
17, 20, 21, 25, 26, 28, 30, 33,
39, 46, 48, 51, 53, 63, 65, 66,
72, 90, 105, 112, 130, 164,
171, 178, 189

James
24, 47, 63, 74, 91, 97, 103, 105,
107, 138, 154

1 Peter
21, 24, 35, 42, 52, 111, 136,
141, 149, 159, 173, 174, 184

2 Peter
29, 56, 119, 177, 190

1 John
20, 58, 71, 97, 101, 108, 114,
154, 192

Revelation
112, 161

Topical Index

Angels, 112

Anger, 20, 34

Attitudes, 20, 89, 155

Becoming like God and Jesus, 50, 163

Bible, The, 46, 118, 134

Church, 135

Committing to God, 52, 81

Courage, 175

Creation, 17, 18, 189

Difficult times, 35, 116

Disobedience, 19, 66, 71, 85, 92, 115

Encourage one another, 72, 125

Faith, 23, 35, 57, 72, 90, 130, 149, 150

Faithfulness, 21

Forgiveness, 36, 97

Fruit of the Spirit, 151

God

    Answers Prayers, 147

    Defeats our enemies, 85

    Forgives, 55

    Protects, 39, 93, 183, 185

    Provides, 45, 52, 143

God's

    Character

        All-knowing, 117

        All-powerful, 17, 28, 33, 67, 106

        Awesome, 46

        Caring, 18

        Greater than all gods, 84

        In control, 22, 41

        Infinite, 83, 103

        King, 86

        Real, 189

        True God, The, 63, 107, 182

        Trustworthy, 45

    Gifts, 48, 74, 102

    Grace, 32, 89, 190

    Help, 40

    Judgment, 29, 41, 44, 115, 119

    Leading, 56, 73

    Love, 154

    Mercy, 124

    Miracles, 44, 56, 64, 67, 109, 110, 178

    Plan, 31, 33, 39, 129, 137, 162, 164

    Promises, 23, 26, 27, 28, 42, 95

    Understanding, 87

    Way, 59, 157

Healing, 111, 117, 142, 149, 153

Heirs of God, 114

Helping others, 126, 154, 158

Holy Spirit, The, 172

Jealousy, 20, 34, 91

Jesus
    As a child, 135
    Blameless, 165
    Cares for us, 138, 142, 143, 148, 150, 158, 177
    Changes us, 176, 182
    Forgives our sins, 144
    God's Son, 133, 152, 171
    Greater than the devil, 136, 146, 167
    Loves everyone, 139, 141, 177
    Only way to God, The, 140
    Our provider, 151
    Passover Lamb, The, 162, 166
    Saves us, 166, 190
    Shows us God, 137
    Suffered for our sins, 164, 165
    Will return, 161
Listening, 82
Living God's way, 191, 192
Love God, 58
Loyalty, 77
Lying, 88
Obedience, 21, 25, 30, 43, 54, 58, 65, 191
Other gods, 49, 71, 84, 92, 104
Patience, 93
Peer pressure, 105
Persecution, 173, 174, 176, 181
Prayer, 51, 101, 103, 147, 153
Pride, 24, 155
Relationships, 57, 77, 180, 192

Responsibility, 123
Salvation, 63, 111, 140, 157, 167, 180
Seek God, 54
Selfishness, 156
Selflessness, 26, 139, 156, 163
Serving God, 126, 179
Sin and Repentance, 19, 29, 66, 96, 97, 108, 144, 145
Talents, 48, 102, 159
Temptation, 74, 96, 136
Ten Commandments, The, 47
Trust, The, 30, 43, 44, 53, 55, 64, 107, 116, 185
Wholehearted, 113
Witnessing, 141, 173, 174, 175, 183, 184
Worship, 49, 51, 94, 160, 181

Welcome to the Family!

Heritage Builders

Helping You Build a Family of Faith

We hope you've enjoyed this book. Heritage Builders was founded in 1995 by three fathers with a passion for the next generation. As a new ministry of Focus on the Family, Heritage Builders strives to equip, train and motivate parents to become intentional about building a strong spiritual heritage.

It's quite a challenge for busy parents to find ways to build a spiritual foundation for their families—especially in a way they enjoy and understand. Through activities and participation, children can learn biblical truth in a way they can understand, enjoy—and *remember*.

Passing along a heritage of Christian faith to your family is a parent's highest calling. Heritage Builders' goal is to encourage and empower you in this great mission with practical resources and inspiring ideas that really work—and help your children develop a lasting love for God.

***

How To Reach Us

For more information, visit our Heritage Builders Web site! Log on to **www.heritagebuilders.com** to discover new resources, sample activities, and ideas to help you pass on a spiritual heritage. To request any of these resources, simply call Focus on the Family at 1-800-A-FAMILY (1-800-232-6459) or in Canada, call 1-800-661-9800. Or send your request to Focus on the Family, Colorado Springs, CO 80995. In Canada, write Focus on the Family, P.O. Box 9800, Stn. Terminal, Vancouver, B.C. V6B 4G3

To learn more about Focus on the Family or to find out if there is an associate office in your country, please visit www. family.org

We'd love to hear from you!

Try These Heritage Builders Resources!

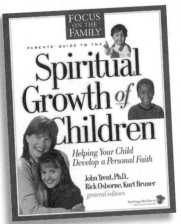

Parents' Guide to the Spiritual Growth of Children

Building a foundation of faith in your children can be easy–and fun!–with help from the *Parents' Guide to the Spiritual Growth of Children*. Through simple and practical advice, this comprehensive guide shows you how to build a spiritual training plan for your family and it explains what to teach your children at different ages.

Bedtime Blessings

Strengthen the precious bond between you, your child and God by making *Bedtime Blessings* a special part of your evenings together. From best-selling author John Trent, Ph.D., and Heritage Builders, this book is filled with stories, activities and blessing prayers to help you practice the biblical model of "blessing."

An Introduction to Family Nights

Make devotions something your children will *never* forget when you involve them in "family nights"—an ideal way to bring fun and spiritual growth together on a weekly basis. *An Introduction to Family Nights* delivers 12 weeks' worth of tried-and-tested ideas and activities for helping kids learn how to tame the tongue, resist temptation, be obedient and much more! Paperback.

Heritage Builders

Helping You Build a Family of Faith

Mealtime Moments

Make your family's time around the dinner table meaningful with *Mealtime Moments,* a book that brings you great discussion starters and activities for teaching your children about your faith. Kids will have fun getting involved with games, trivia questions and theme nights, all based on spiritually sound ideas. Perfect for the whole family! Spiralbound.

Joy Ride!

Use your drive time to teach your kids how faith can be part of everyday life with *Joy Ride!* A wonderful resource for parents, this book features activities, puzzles, games and discussion starters to help get your kids thinking about—and living out—what they believe.

• • •

Visit our Heritage Builders Web site! Log on to **www.heritagebuilders.com** to discover new resources, sample activities, and ideas to help you pass on a spiritual heritage. To request any of these resources, simply call Focus on the Family at 1-800-A-FAMILY (1-800-232-6459) or in Canada, call 1-800-661-9800. Or send your request to Focus on the Family, Colorado Springs, CO 80995. In Canada, write Focus on the Family, P.O. Box 9800, Stn. Terminal, Vancouver, B.C. V6B 4G3.

Heritage
Builders

Helping You Build a Family of Faith

Every family has a heritage—a spiritual, emotional, and social legacy passed from one generation to the next. There are four main areas we at Heritage Builders recommend parents consider as they plan to pass their faith to their children:

Family Fragrance

Every family's home has a fragrance. Heritage Builders encourages parents to create a home environment that fosters a sweet, Christ-centered AROMA of love through Affection, Respect, Order, Merriment, and Affirmation.

Family Traditions

Whether you pass down stories, beliefs and/or customs, traditions can help you establish a special identity for your family. Heritage Builders encourages parents to set special "milestones" for their children to help guide them and move them through their spiritual development.

Family Compass

Parents have the unique task of setting standards for normal, healthy living through their attitudes, actions and beliefs. Heritage Builders encourages parents to give their children the moral navigation tools they need to succeed on the roads of life.

Family Moments

Creating special, teachable moments with their children is one of a parent's most precious and sometimes, most difficult responsibilities. Heritage Builders encourages parents to capture little moments throughout the day to teach and impress values, beliefs, and biblical principles onto their children.

We look forward to standing alongside you as you seek to impart the Lord's care and wisdom onto the next generation—onto your children.

Heritage
Builders

Helping You Build a Family of Faith

LIGHT wave
building Christian faith in families

Lightwave Publishing is one of North America's leading developers of quality resources that encourage, assist, and equip parents to build Christian faith in their families. Their products help parents answer their children's questions about the Christian faith, teach them how to make church, Sunday school, and Bible reading more meaningful for their children, provide them with pointers on teaching their children to pray, and much, much more.

Lightwave, together with its various publishing and ministry partners, such as Focus on the Family, has been successfully producing innovative books, music, and games for the past 15 years. Some of their more recent products include the *Parents' Guide to the Spiritual Growth of Children*, *Mealtime Moments*, and *Joy Ride!*.

Lightwave also has a fun kids' web site and an Internet-based newsletter called *Tips and Tools for Spiritual Parenting*. For more information and a complete list of Lightwave products, please visit: **www.lightwavepublishing.com**.